CONCISE COLLEGE TEXTS

THE MAKING
OF
BUSINESS CONTRACTS

AUSTRALIA
The Law Book Company Ltd.
Sydney: Melbourne: Brisbane

CANADA AND U.S.A.
The Carswell Company Ltd.
Agincourt, Ontario

INDIA
N. M. Tripathi Private Ltd.
Bombay

ISRAEL
Steimatzky's Agency Ltd.
Jerusalem: Tel Aviv: Haifa

MALAYSIA : SINGAPORE : BRUNEI
Malayan Law Journal (Pte.) Ltd.
Singapore

NEW ZEALAND
Sweet and Maxwell (N.Z.) Ltd.
Wellington

PAKISTAN
Pakistan Law House
Karachi

CONCISE COLLEGE

THE MAKING

OF

BUSINESS CONTRACTS

BY

A. HARDING BOULTON, LL.B., F.C.I.S.

SECOND EDITION

LONDON

First Edition (1965) *by* A. Harding Boulton
Second Edition (1972) *by* A. Harding Boulton

Published in 1972 *by*
Sweet & Maxwell Limited of
11 *New Fetter Lane, London,*
and printed in Great Britain
by The Devonshire Press Ltd.,
Barton Road, Torquay

SBN   Hardback   421 15320 2
Paperback   421 15330 X

PREFACE TO FIRST EDITION

THIS book is an attempt to break new ground. It is concerned with the twilit borderland where the law and the practice of industry and commerce meet and sometimes overlap. The underlying motif of the greater part of the book could be indicated by suggesting as a sub-title " How to Read (and Write) the Small Type on the Back."

Certainly no apology is needed for offering a book on this subject. The vast majority of the contracts involved in industry and commerce other than those in the retail trade are governed by more or less stereotyped conditions which are not subjected to critical scrutiny as often as they might be. The purpose of this book is to help the business executive to see these documents in their right perspective and to read them with discernment. That it might have been a much more exhausive study if the author had been able to devote more time to its compilation is certain. It is equally certain that it could have been a much better book if he had been gifted with greater ability. Such as it is, however, it is offered to the reader in the hope that it will be found of interest and some value.

The author acknowledges his indebtedness to the many anonymous draftsmen who have provided him with illustrations. Where these are used merely for the purposes of illustration, and especially where they are made the subject of critical comment, it has not been thought desirable to indicate their source. They are, however, all entirely authentic.

The book is necessarily selective, and is coloured by the author's experience in the engineering industry. If there is bias, it is probably towards sympathy for the manufacturer.

In the latter part of the book suggestions are made regarding the content of certain typical forms of agreement familiar in the conduct of business relations. In these chapters the intention has not been to offer any forms of precedents nor to criticise existing precedents, but to assist the business executive to clarify his thoughts before preparing his contract, or, in the alternative, instructing his lawyers regarding the points which are to be covered.   The matter they contain is the fruit of experience rather than of theory.

The author also gratefully acknowledges the permission given by the British Electrical and Allied Manufacturers Association, the Institution of Electrical Engineers, and the Purchasing Officers Association for the reproduction of standard sets of conditions of sale and purchase.

A. HARDING BOULTON

PREFACE TO SECOND EDITION

IN offering a second edition of this book the opportunity has been taken to introduce a number of minor changes which, it is hoped, will enhance its value to the student of Management. Notice has been taken of statutes passed since the preparation of the first edition, including the Misrepresentation Act 1967 and the Trade Descriptions Act 1968. A section has been introduced dealing with the special features of hire purchase contracts, one with the special considerations applying to the international carriage of goods. A short chapter has been added dealing with price variations, and a longer one briefly reviewing the nature of the contract of insurance. Finally, because this work is aimed particularly at the student of business and management studies to whom the quotation of case reports tends to be a mystery, a brief note about legal case references follows the Preface.

A. HARDING BOULTON

A NOTE ABOUT LEGAL CASE REFERENCES

IT is customary, when quoting a legal case, to append a reference by which anyone wishing to follow out more critically the point it illustrates may find it. Although readers of this book are not, on the whole, likely to wish to do this, these references have been given. They follow a recognised pattern, thus—

Edwards *v.* Skyways Ltd. [1964] 1 W.L.R. 349
Williams *v.* Fitzmaurice (1858) 3 M. & N. 844

This means that in the first case the plaintiff was Edwards and the defendant Skyways Ltd., and in the second, the plaintiff Williams and the defendant Fitzmaurice. The years in which the cases were contested are shown in the bracket. The rest of the reference is an indication of the series of reports and the page number where it may be found.

Before 1865, when the Incorporated Council of Law Reporting was formed, the reports were private ventures, and, as such, patchy in extent and quality. As one goes back, they are increasingly brief and selective. Law reports are available in public libraries only in major cities. Such libraries as that of the Guildhall or the City of Westminister carry fairly complete sets, as do the Universities possessing faculties of law, and, for later years, the professional institutes serving the accountancy and secretarial professions. The Law Society and the Inns of Court naturally seek to be exhaustive, and, as a courtesy, will generally allow non-members to examine a book if approached. Otherwise, the British Museum Library remains as a last resource.

The following explains the abbreviations used. Dates, where given, indicate the periods which the series covers.

A.C.	Appeal Court
All E.R.	All England Reports
App. Cas.	Law Reports—Appeal Cases
C.P.D.	Law Reports, Common Pleas Division
E.R.	English Reports
Ex.	Exchequer Reports
	(Welsby, Murestone & Gordon)
H. & N.	Hurlstone and Norman's Reports

H.L. Cas.	Clark's Reports, House of Lords
K.B.	King's Bench
Lloyd's Rep.	Lloyd's List Law Reports
M. & W.	Meeson and Welsby's Reports 1836–1847
Q.B.	Queen's Bench
Q.B.D.	Queen's Bench Division
T.L.R.	*Times* Law Reports
W.L.R.	Weekly Law Reports

CONTENTS

PART ONE

STANDARD FORM CONTRACTS

PART TWO

OTHER COMMERCIAL CONTRACTS

CASES REFERRED TO IN THE TEXT

STATUTES REFERRED TO IN TEXT

Part 1
STANDARD FORM CONTRACTS

Chapter 1

INTRODUCTION—THE LEGAL FUNCTION IN BUSINESS

THERE are many books on the law of contract. They differ widely in sophistication and usefulness, ranging from great classics used by the practitioner, written, rewritten, and annotated by successive editors and revisers long after their original and illustrious authors are dead, to the elementary textbooks designed to do little more than to assist the young student over his first hurdles when preparing for the intermediate examination for a commercial qualification. Into this wide field this book is not designed to trespass; its purpose may be defined as being to provide practical assistance to those who, not being lawyers, are yet responsible for exercising the legal function in business.

The phrase " the legal function in business " as used here calls for some explanation, and in the course of the explanation the scope and purpose of the book will become clearer. It is an evident fact that commercial life consists of the making and fulfilling of contracts, using the word " contract " in its true sense as meaning any agreement designed to create obligations enforceable at law. Almost every act in business life creates legal rights and duties; the right to receive benefits, the duty to pay for them, the duty to supply goods or services, the right to be paid. As business goes on in its accustomed way, the fact that it consists of this web of legal rights and duties may not occupy the forefront of our minds. Indeed, it is good that it should not, for it would be intolerable to live our business lives always thinking of the precise legal obligations which press upon us at every moment of the day, and perhaps worse to be engrossed always in the definition and exaction of our precisely determined rights. It is good that the necessarily rigid and narrow concepts of legal rights and duties should be hidden from immediate view by the zest for activity, the stimulus of the rough and tumble of competition, and by the equivalent, in this machine age, of the joy a craftsman feels in achievement. But the fact of rights and duties is never very far away in the background. It is desirable, indeed imperative, that legal rights and duties should be always recognised as underlying

1

the daily activity, underpinning and giving strength to the structure of business. Because this is so, it is important that they should indeed be what they are imagined to be, that they should possess the strength and precision they are assumed to have. The first requirement for the prevention of disputes is that each party should know what the rights and obligations of both parties to a contract are, and that they should never proceed on the basis of merely vague ideas of what is required, each thinking differently from the other and acting accordingly. From time to time, when things go awry, when goods are defective or due payments are not made, when the good fellowship evaporates from the daily give and take of commercial relationship, the legal rights will be invoked and the strength of the structure that lies behind the façade of business enthusiasm and bonhomie will come to the test.

The businessman tends to adopt an ambivalent view towards the law and lawyers. He is desperately anxious to be able to insist upon his legal rights if he has need so to do, while hating to be thought to adopt a " legalistic " attitude. He views lawyers with some degree of awe, touched with affection when it is his own lawyer who is the subject, and with dislike and suspicion when other people's lawyers are concerned. His own lawyer is the man to whom he repairs readily enough when trouble is upon him, when litigation threatens, when debtors are neglectful or creditors unyielding. But at other times he feels that the lawyer is some-what remote from the facts of life as indeed, in one sense, he is and knows himself to be. Sometimes when he discusses with other businessmen arrangements which he seeks to enter into with them, especially in the early stages of negotiations, he is very ready to suggest " let's keep the lawyers out of this." He feels, not always without some justification, that the presence of the lawyer in business discussion can operate as a brake or create inhibitions or suspicions. He refers to the language which lawyers use in their documents as legal " jargon " or " verbiage " and is rather contemptuous of it, and may be heard to refer in general and disparaging terms to the "small type on the back " of some printed document by which he will bind or be bound.

The reason for this is very easy to understand. It is that the law involves not only a certain body of knowledge, but a way of thinking, and that way of thinking is not one easy to enter into in the occasional enthusiasms and the frequent dull routines of business life. It is the habit of the lawyer to ask for precision. There is a stage of negotiation when the time is not right for precision, and at that stage the lawyer's presence may be unwelcome. His habit of analysis causes him to be suspect when the attention of those who have business in hand is engrossed with imaginative forward thinking. When the businessman is in trouble, however, he goes to his lawyer, and if he is wise he will go readily when the first lineaments of trouble are discerned. He consults the lawyer readily enough, too, when the problems he faces are of particular magnitude or of an unfamiliar quality.

Passing down the scale of business transactions from the negotiation of major contracts and the facing of crises, there are a number of transactions at the other end which occur so frequently and are of such a routine nature that nothing at all appears in writing in connection with them and the facts that they create legal rights and duties is hardly remembered. The greater part of the retail trade comes within this category. Without any specific contract in writing and perhaps no contract in spoken words (as in a self-service store) these contracts are such that the need to define any legal rights and duties does not arise in one case in a thousand and when it does can well be left to the common law.

Between the two extremes represented, on the one hand, by the contract sufficiently important or complex for the lawyers to be consulted, and on the other, those which are so frequent or of such a routine nature as to be treated casually with hardly any recognition that they involve a contractual operation at all, lie innumerable intermediate contracts which make up a large part of daily business life. They can involve important questions and, indeed, can give rise to consequences that can break or make a business, but in their formation the lawyer is not normally consulted. The ordering of goods, the acceptance of orders for goods, the carriage of goods, agreements for agencies, building and structural engineering contracts, the employment of staff – all these are for the most part contracts which are not taken to the lawyers for negotiation, and it will usually be found that within the business itself some person (or persons) may exercise the " legal function " in respect of these arrangements.

It may be exercised only very loosely, but generally the responsibility of reading the documents by which such contracts are entered into, or of settling their form when they originate within the business itself, will be found to rest upon some executive or to be dispersed amongst a limited number of people. Not infrequently the company secretary carries the responsibility, or it may be a manager or managing director or contract manager or, within their own functional operations, the buyer or sales manager. Almost certainly the function will be exercised in a way that merges it with other duties, and for this reason it may be done very imperfectly. It may never be clearly visualised as the important function it is. If, however, in a business of any magnitude there is no competent person available to look at the transactions of the undertaking from a legal point of view, it is easy for trouble to lurk unseen. It may be found, for example, that when it is desired to sue another undertaking for breach of contract, scrutiny of the facts and the papers by lawyers may disclose that there never was a contract to break, or perhaps, even more exasperating, the contract was unwittingly entered into in words originating from the other side which completely erode the case on which it is desired to initiate action.

If, however, this function is performed properly many dangers will be avoided. It should be envisaged clearly and allotted to an executive with adequate intelligence and training. It is becoming increasingly common for the larger company to take a solicitor or barrister into its staff, and often indeed, to create a separate legal department which operates almost as a professional firm. The degree to which such a department is consulted varies, as does its effective authority. But smaller businesses cannot afford this luxury: only a really large undertaking can justify the expense, or provide the steady load of worthwhile work without which a professionally qualified person will not be satisfied even though he be adequately paid. For this reason it is right that in the training afforded to those who aspire to office as business executives some instruction in the general principles of law is normally included. The qualifying examinations of the professional associations issuing qualifications in accountancy, secretaryship, and other business skills normally include papers on those branches of the law which seem most relevant to the respective avocations.

Knowledge gained in order to pass a necessarily elementary examination is not always to the point, however. Business transactions are tending to be increasingly integrated into routine procedures, achieved through the use of printed forms, standard conditions and the like. The classical cases which still properly find their places in the elementary textbooks, cases about horses that kick, the painting of coach doors, and the inevitable snail in the bottle are remote from the present world, though the principles they illustrate remain valid. There is need to supplement the basic knowledge imparted by the elementary textbook of contract law by some illustrations of the way in which some typical contracts are entered into in practice, of the place and purpose of common form contracts. In brief there is need for guidance as to what to look for in the " small type on the back." In the last resort nothing can take the place of experience, but the value of experience can be enhanced by guidance. There is no quality so valuable in business nor perhaps any so rare as the ability to be prompt, reliable and firm in judgment, and any help towards the development of this quality is well given and received. All of us know how valuable is the rare quality possessed by just a few men and women, the ability to take a swift grasp of essentials and to detect, almost at a glance, the nub of a problem, bringing simplicity out of confusion. Such a quality is, indeed, a natural gift, but this is not to say that it can never be cultivated.

The scope of this book is, then, to help those who, not being lawyers, are in day-to-day contact with the texture of business and have to exercise the legal function in relation to the daily flux of affairs. In the exercise of this function they need to show common sense and qualities of sound judgment. The book will not deal with the common law aspects of the kind of transaction that is not evidenced by writing, nor, on the other hand, with the kind of contract in connection with which solicitors are customarily consulted at the time when it is made. It is concerned with a group of typical contracts which lie between the two. It is a broad terrain very fruitful in disputes and misunderstandings and as such is one which can and does provide much raw material for litigation.

No attempt has been made to be exhaustive, for to cover the whole field of commercial contracts would not only require many volumes but would also call for a team of experts. The contracts concerned are those relating to the buying and selling of goods, the construction of buildings, civil engineering works and erection of machinery, the carriage of goods, agencies and distributorships, patent licences and know-how agreements, insurance, import and export, and agreements relating to employment. Finally, a brief chapter offers advice on the drafting of those agreements which need to be individually written.

That such a book should be offered, it is believed for the first time in England, is itself symptomatic of a change which has taken place within the present century. This change is to some degree the consequence of the increasing size and complexity of the business unit. It is also due to the desire and the ability of a growing number of people to see the economic operation as a whole and to see it intelligently, which is at once the cause and effect of the academic study of business and economic affairs. The change is that the boundary between law and business is becoming blurred. Until the latter part of the last century, the law operated within its own enclave of mystery, whilst each craft and trade had its own mystery, its own traditions, secrets and vocabulary. The gulf between the attorney's office and the merchant's counting-house was wide. Now the legal profession is finding itself increasingly engaged in the day-to-day business of trade and industry, and conversely, the business executive is put to the necessity of understanding more and more of the law. There is nothing inappropriate in all this, for, as the lawyers are only too ready to point out to us, ignorance of the law is of no value as an excuse for breaking it. Since, therefore, no bliss is found in this kind of ignorance, there is no folly in being wise.

CHAPTER 2

THE SALE AND PURCHASE OF GOODS

1. The function of conditions of sale

It is evident that the contract for the sale of goods is the most basic of all the contracts of commerce. It goes back to the dawn of history and every legal system has had to take cognisance of it and to provide rules by which it should be controlled and interpreted. In the case of English law, however, it was only in the Sale of Goods Act 1893 that any comprehensive code was written to define the rights and duties of the buyer and seller of goods. Until then the contract was regulated and interpreted by the unwritten common law, which had itself emerged from the customs observed and recognised in the various fairs and markets over the centuries. These local rules and practices had gradually become assimilated to a common standard, and the purpose of the legislature in 1893 was not to make any change in the law but to set out in a formulated code a statement of the law as it then existed.

Since 1893, other statutes have been enacted which bear upon the matter of buying and selling. The most important are the Trade Descriptions Act 1968, the Misrepresentation Act 1967 and the Hire Purchase Acts 1938–65. The last mentioned deal with the conduct of a vast field of business which had hardly been dreamed of in 1893.

The contract of sale must therefore be viewed against the background of these statutes. Numerically the vast majority of sales of goods are made in the retail market, without being evidenced by any written record, and in respect of most of these sales the provisions of the Acts apply without modification. When, however, one passes out of the field of retail trade and examines the purchase and sale of goods in the practical conduct of industry, the sales made by manufacturers to wholesalers or the purchases made by professional buyers, it is usual to find that the contract of sale or purchase is not to be interpreted solely by the provisions of the Sale of Goods Act and the other statutes mentioned, but by a set of " conditions " put forward by one party or the other.   Often it is necessary to consider the effect of two sets of conditions, one put forward by each party, and not fully consistent with each other.   The contract of sale may therefore be of some complexity, and only capable of being construed when a number of documents have been studied and reconciled.   The purpose of this chapter is to consider why such documents should be used at all and what it is that those who create them seek to achieve.

In English law the principle is recognised that in the contract of sale the parties are free to make their own bargain, subject to any limitations imposed upon them by the general law.   There are, of course, some special cases and special circumstances limiting this freedom, as, for example, the special requirements in connection with hire-purchase contracts, and those restrictions which applied during the war period and its aftermath when rationing and price regulation were extensive.   In general terms, however, it is clear from the wording of the Sale of Goods Act itself, that the principle of freedom to contract is paramount, so that the place of the Act is not to force the contract of sale into any rigid pattern, but to provide a background and to furnish a set of rules which can be applied where the parties either have not entered into a detailed contract or have not, in their own contract, provided for some eventuality.

To the question whether " conditions of sale " are necessary, the answer is therefore that they are not, provided the parties to the transaction are satisfied to leave their contract to be interpreted in all respects by the Sale of Goods Act and the general law. The possible reasons for the proliferation of these documents may therefore be summed up as:

(a)   The belief that a code written three-quarters of a century ago is not suited to the conditions of trading at the present day.

(b)   A desire to avoid or modify in some way the consequences which would flow from the acceptance of the Act and general law as regulating the contract.

(c)   The fact that to put forward one's own conditions is the most tactful and practical method of refusing to accept those of the other party, which may prejudice the contract against one's own interest.

(d)   The tendency to copy others.

This last mentioned reason was commented upon by Sir Patrick Devlin (now Lord Devlin) in a lecture given in 1951:

> " The ordinary small tradesman sometimes has a set of conditions on the back of his notepaper. He rarely takes the necessary precautions to make sure they are part of any contract; and certainly never envisages the possibility of their clashing with a similar set of conditions on the other side. A fortnight ago a witness before me, who found himself in that position, was asked why he had not written to the other side so as to reach some agreement upon what conditions should prevail. ' We should never get any business done if we did that sort of thing,' he said, ' besides, we haven't got time for it.' ' Then why do you have any conditions at all? ' ' Oh, everybody does.' Usually such conditions have grown up piecemeal. On an occasion when he sustains some reverse at the hands of the law, the businessman will decide that he must have something to prevent that happening again and will frame a condition accordingly."

This comment was based upon his long experience of commercial litigation and is undoubtedly true. The formulation of new clauses in the circumstances described has come more and more into the province of trade associations rather than the individual trader, and the activities of the associations have made it easier for the individual trader to fall into fashion like the litigant who had conditions because " everybody does." However this may be, such documents exist by the thousand, and as a result it is not infrequently necessary to do one's best to spell out a contract from various documents which purport to reflect the minds of the parties but whose content is often known only vaguely even to the party putting them forward, and which the other may not have read at all. Often they are printed in minute print on the back of flimsy forms and are almost impossible to read. Contracts involving large sums of money rest legally upon a welter of paper and are never reduced to the order that a lawyer would like to see. Fortunately most of them reach a satisfactory fulfilment without litigation or even dispute.

The third of the reasons mentioned above needs little comment. It will clearly emerge in the course of this chapter that to accept the conditions put forward by some buyers or sellers could place the other party at an unfair disadvantage. Merely to reject is difficult; especially as the existence of the Sale of Goods Act as a code lying in the background is not always appreciated by buyers and sellers. The fact that " everybody " has conditions would render unacceptable the suggestion that conditions put forward by one party can be rejected by the other without anything being substituted, and therefore the existence of some document to put forward as an alternative, even if only to enable a compromise to be reached, is a practical necessity.

The first and second reasons given for the creation of these documents are, however, more solid and merit attention. The Sale of Goods Act itself bears the date 1893, but it represented a codification of the law as it had been defined during the preceding centuries, and especially the nineteenth century. It is noteworthy that many of the classical cases still quoted in books on the sale of goods, the cases which provided the law of which the Act was a codification, belonged to the first three-quarters of the nineteenth century. It is clear from the nature of the transactions with which these cases were concerned that commerce during that period was very much more truly a matter of merchanting than it is today. Merchants bought and sold produce and wares using their skill and judgment, being appealed to by buyers for their recommendations, prospering or failing according to their acumen in trading, their skill in understanding the materials they handled, and the reputations they achieved. Manufacture was far simpler than it is today. There was little or no national advertising, no packaging industry, few nationally known brand names, and no system of standard specifications.

There is no need to elaborate the many technical, economic and social changes that have transformed the business world since then. It is sufficient to point out that a distribution industry has largely displaced the whole network of merchanting which then existed, while on the technical side, the effect of technological change on the practice of business may be illustrated by trying to interpret, with no assistance but the Sale of Goods Act and the common law, the after-sales obligations of the manufacturer of a computer installation.

It is, however, the second-mentioned reason, that is to say, the desire to modify the terms of the contract of sale away from the standard set by the provisions of the Act, which underlies most of the more common provisions of the conditions of sale drawn up and used in contemporary commerce, and it is with this aspect that the next section of this chapter will be concerned. It is easy to understand why this should be so. Traditionally the maxim *caveat emptor* suggested that under the common law any advantage of interpretation would be likely to lie with the seller. In so far as this might be so it is natural for the buyer to seek to impose expressly terms that will give him protection. On the other hand, some sections of the Act embody principles by which the decisions of the courts had eroded the old maxim, and in consequence the Act does in fact lay some very onerous obligations upon the seller, and he on his part will seek to limit their application. Both buyer and seller therefore, under the overriding principle that the contract of sale is a consensual contract in which the parties are free to make their own bargains, are perfectly within their rights in negotiating each for his own advantage, and it is interesting to see how the conditions written by or in the interest of the buyer or seller, as the case may be, can become a battle of wits around their opposed desires, united in wishing to modify the basic principles upheld by the Sale of Goods Act, but opposed in their choice of the points at which or the degree to which this is to be done. Sometimes it can clearly be seen that some basic principle is accepted by each, but that in embodying it in his conditions the one will seek to widen it and the other to narrow it.

In the main, conditions of sale have been evolved by the seller. There is good reason for this. The special considerations which cause the bare statute law of the Sale of Goods Act to be unsuited to a particular class of goods appeal primarily to and are best understood by the manufacturers of these goods. Sellers, apart from those in retail trade, are usually specialists, buyers on the other hand generally have to buy over a wide range of products, touching many industries. Any set of conditions designed by a buyer is therefore likely to be very general in its application. This does not, however, mean that the seller has it all his own way. Sometimes the buyer is sufficiently influential to insist on his own terms, and then the modifications made to the statutory norm provided by the Sale of Goods Act are in the opposite direction.

The fact is that the whole situation tends to give rise to a jungle of verbiage, and any industrial buyer or seller conscientious enough to read all the terms and conditions upon which goods or orders are offered to him, zealous enough to argue about all their unreasonableness, and pertinacious enough to follow through his arguments to a negotiated conclusion, would probably attain for himself little except an early grave. He would not even serve his own organisation very well, for his zeal would so slow down the tempo of life that his store or factory would be hamstrung for want of supplies or shortage of orders. The best he can hope for is to make such endeavour as is reasonably possible through his order forms to impose some reasonable safeguards, to challenge the more extreme provisions which other parties seek on their part to impose upon him, and to negotiate a comprehensive agreement on terms and conditions with those with whom he has most extensive dealings.

Scrutiny of the sets of conditions which are to be found in the course of buying and selling in commerce and industry soon shows that they fall into a few recognisable groups:

(a) Those which are drafted in the interest of the seller, usually a manufacturer, and which are quite evidently written in his interest.

(b) Those which are drafted in the interest of the buyer, and which he seeks to impose.

(c) Those which are the work of professional associations which stand in a position to hold the scales with reasonable impartiality between the buyer and the seller.

(d) Those which are written for use by government departments and other public authorities, mostly when operating as buyers. These tend to be fairer than (b) and are much more expertly written.

(e) Those which are written for the buying departments of very large undertakings, and which, because of the public standing of their sponsors, are less biased than (b) but not quite so fair as (d).

One is tempted to comment that, especially in clauses (a) and (b), another division is possible, that is to say:

(i) Those which are written by lawyers and though perfectly precise to other lawyers are not always comprehensible to the layman.

(ii) Those which are written by intelligent laymen for other intelligent men and which, though not always possessing the legal precision of (i) can be understood by most people.

(iii) Those which are written by the incompetent and cannot be understood at all.

The question whether it is in the interest of business relationships for conditions of contract to be drafted by lawyers or laymen is an interesting one. It is significant that on balance and whilst recognising the disadvantages, Devlin L.J., in the lecture referred to earlier in this chapter, expressed the view that the balance of advantage lay with the practice of businessmen writing their own conditions.

" It may seem curious that when the authors of these forms and clauses realise, as they must, that in the event of a dispute the result will turn upon what view the lawyer takes of them, they should not get a lawyer to draft them. But they regard it as more important that they should keep the drafting in their own hands, and I think that, whatever the formal imperfections may be, it is a practice which contributes to the health and vitality of commercial law. Although it may not render the corpus of commercial law more beautiful or more artistic, it does make it healthier and more vigorous."

In the course of this study reference will be made by way of illustration to a number of clauses actually found in various sets of conditions of contract of sale or purchase. By way of full illustration of the several types mentioned in the first and more serious classification above, reference may now be made to some typical examples.

The Conditions of Sale A of the British Electrical and Allied Manufacturers Association, stated to be applicable to the " Sale of Goods for use in the United Kingdom, exclusive of erection " constitute an excellent example of the conditions framed in the interest of the manufacturing seller. That some of the conditions are necessary is very clear. The members of the Association manufacture a range of finished goods, few of which had ever been heard of in 1893. To be left with the Sale of Goods Act as a code for application to such sales would involve a host of difficulties. Quite evidently, however, they do not stand between the parties as an attempt to be impartial; in clause after clause

they are designed to protect the selling manufacturer from obligations which in their absence he might be left to bear. With the
exception of the patent indemnity clause, they do not set out to lay
obligations on the seller nor to protect the legitimate interests of
the buyer. It is, however, only fair to note that the Association
recommends its members to accept as an alternative, if so
requested, the impartial and professionally sponsored conditions
of the Institute of Electrical Engineers, and does not object to the
buyer-orientated conditions of the Purchasing Officers Association.[1]

The order forms used by buying departments are often
covered with small type conditions which upon examination prove
to be biased in the opposite direction. The extent of their bias
varies from a natural emphasis in the buyer's interest to sheer
unreasonableness. A reasoned approach which does not make
any outrageous demand upon the seller, but is clearly designed in
the interest of the buyer is found in the conditions recommended
by the Purchasing Officers Association. These, because designed
for general use, are very broad based, and comparison with
B.E.A.M.A. " A " show not only the difference between buyer
and seller-orientated conditions but also the way in which sellers'
conditions are more specialised than those prepared for use by
buyers.

The approach of the professional association is well illustrated
by the Model Conditions C published jointly by the Institutions
of Electrical and Mechanical Engineers. The Institutions are
professional societies whose members cover the interests of manufacturers, users, technologists and consultants. As these are
designed to be applied *inter alia* to the same range of products
as are the conditions of the B.E.A.M.A., an interesting comparison
may be made of the two sets.

2. Deviations from the Sale of Goods Act

In the light of the foregoing, attention will now be given to
some of the typical provisions of the standard sets of conditions,
to illustrate the way in which the respective interests of the seller
and buyer lead to modifications being made in the standard contract of sale which would exist if the transaction were left solely

---

[1] The Purchasing Officers Association is now incorporated into the Institute of
Purchasing and Supply. The conditions used for illustration, however, ante-
date the merger of associations which led to the formation of the Institute.

to the provisions of the Sale of Goods Act. The subjects which are introduced for special consideration are selected not only as typical but as constituting the most important of the attempted deviations in practice.

(i) *Definition of the contract*

As a general principle it will be universally agreed that the more precisely one can define the provisions of a contract the better, and it is desirable to be able to limit with certainty the documents which are to be examined in order to establish those provisions. This is not to say, however, that in any given contractual situation the parties will agree where the limit is to be drawn.

The Act does not give a great deal of assistance, and one is led back to the general law of contract, and to the necessity of defining a point at which it is possible to construe the documentation as constituting an offer and an acceptance of that offer. If, as often happens, the actual contract of sale comes at the end of a long period of negotiation in which a number of representations have been made regarding the goods, sometimes in an express and specific form, and sometimes by means of general statements in advertising media, it tends to be to the advantage of the buyer to regard all these representations as being germane to the contract, whereas it is to the advantage of the seller to set a clear limit to the number of documents that are to be relied upon. It is clearly established that unless the immediate terms of the contract expressly provide to the contrary a representation regarding the goods made by the seller before the sale, and designed to influence the buyer towards entering into the contract, is a condition of the contract. This doctrine has been recently extended by the courts,[2] so that a buyer may be able to sue a manufacturer on a representation made by him regarding the goods sold by a distributor notwithstanding that the contract of sale was not made with the manufacturer but with the distributor.

The law has for a long time recognised that a distinction exists between a mere commendation of goods for the purpose of advertisement and a representation made in order to induce a buyer. Under the contemptuous expression " a mere puff " much of the output of the contemporary art of advertising may be

[2] *Wells (Merstham)* v. *Buckland Sand and Silica Co.* [1965] 2 Q.B. 170.

dismissed. No action would lie at the instance of an aggrieved buyer who complained that a detergent advertised as washing " whiter than white " did no more than wash white, if only because it would be difficult to give any meaning to the phrase. But it is far from easy to determine exactly at what point a statement ceases to be a mere advertising commendation and becomes a representation to be imported into the contract.

The matter becomes more complicated when the goods of sale are technical products. The typical selling transaction today, outside the range of the retail market, takes place between the sales representative of manufacturing industry and the commercial buyer. In the case of technical products the commercial buyer may have to refer to specialists on his own side whose expertise is involved, and on the seller's side the transaction may move from the sales representative to the technologist. Not infrequently the final stage is the evolution of a specification by negotiation between the parties. Over the course of the negotiations the seller may be represented at different times by different persons whose authority to make representations on his behalf may not be very clearly defined – and in this respect it is the representative's apparent authority that matters more than his real authority – so that it is possible for a number of assertions to be made as to the quality of the goods and in the case of machinery as to its anticipated performance. There may also be a wealth of published material in the shape of catalogues, specifications, and the like, all of which may be regarded as having influenced the buyer.

In view of this it is in the interest of the seller to make sure that, at the point of time at which the contract is entered into, all irrelevant and casual statements regarding the goods are clearly excluded from the scope of the contract proper. Thus in the typical B.E.A.M.A. " A " conditions:

> All specifications, drawings and particulars of weights and dimensions submitted with our tender are approximate only, and the descriptions and illustrations contained in our catalogues, price lists and other advertisement matter are intended merely to present a general idea of the goods described therein, and none of these shall form part of the contract. After acceptance of our tender a set of certified outline drawings will be supplied free of charge on request.

This clause is skilfully drawn. It will be noted that it excludes from the scope of the contract particulars " submitted with " the tender, and contained in the more general sales literature, but does not exclude particulars that may be *contained in* the tender, to do which would be unreasonable. In the interpretation of a contract governed by a clause of this kind it may therefore be important to determine whether a specification or drawing is " submitted with " the tender or is an integral part of the tender, a distinction which can be easily overlooked. There are practical reasons why, especially to a manufacturer of technical products which are in the course of constant development and refinement, such a safeguard is necessary. It is not practicable, every time some technical change of a minor type is made, for a complete scrutiny of all extant sales literature to be made and alterations effected in order to bring the literature into line with practice. However, the question must sometimes arise how far the protection which such a clause purports to give is reasonable. The wise buyer of a technical product will seek some assurance and guarantee of its specification and performance in a form that will bring it within the substantive contract, and will take steps to ensure that everything he has been told about the goods he is buying will not be arbitrarily excluded from the contract by such a clause.

It is not usual to find any clause matching this in conditions which buyers seek to impose. Naturally the interests of the buyer are best served by leaving the matter open so that any of the seller's negotiating representations can be relied upon. Buyers' conditions naturally tend to throw the emphasis upon the order as the ruling document without, however, expressly excluding other documents. Thus the Purchasing Officers Association conditions provide:

. . . the goods shall
- (i) conform, as to quantity, quality and description with the particulars stated in the order,
- (ii) be of sound materials and workmanship,
- (iii) be equal in all respects to the samples, patterns or specifications provided or given by either party.

The conditions put forward by a United Kingdom nationalised industry are of interest in this connection.

> The Articles shall be of the qualities and sorts described and equal in all respects to the Specifications, Patterns, Drawings and Samples which form part of the Contract Documents *or are otherwise relevant for the purposes of the Contract . . . .*[3]

The words italicised can open the door to a great deal of argument, and would seem to be wide enough to include practically any express statement regarding the goods.

The Misrepresentation Act 1967 introduced into the law of contract a provision which limited the effect of any attempt to exclude from the contract anything outside the contract documents themselves, as is done in the B.E.A.M.A. clause quoted above. In sections 1 and 2 it introduced a simplification in the law of contract by which the somewhat artificial distinction between "condition" and "warranty" became of no practical effect, and provided that a party induced to enter into a contract by misrepresentation, whether made innocently or fraudulently, was to have the right to rescind the contract or to claim damages. It then proceeded in section 3 to render ineffective any provision by which the parties purported to contract out of the effect of the Act. It therefore follows that if, in fact, goods are purchased on the basis of statements made by the vendor and believed by the purchaser, any provision in the contract itself which, by excluding anything not contained in the contract documents themselves, purports to relieve the vendor from the consequences of any earlier misrepresentation is liable to be overruled. The Trade Descriptions Act 1968 carried this principle farther by rendering the making of false or misleading descriptions of goods in advertising or other descriptive matter a penal offence.

(ii) *Suitability for a purpose*

The position under the Sale of Goods Act regarding the suitability of goods for the purpose for which they have been acquired is set out in section 14 (1):

> "Where the buyer, expressly or by implication, makes known to the seller the particular purpose for which the goods are required, so as to show that the buyer relies on the seller's skill or judgment, and the goods are of a description

[3] United Kingdom Atomic Energy Authority.

which it is the course of the seller's business to supply (whether he be the manufacturer or not) there is an implied condition that the goods shall be reasonably fit for such purpose."

This, as a general statement of the law, is well accepted as reasonable, and both sellers and buyers readily recognise it. It is interesting to note, however, how the seller hedges it round and limits its application, whilst the buyer seeks to extend it. Thus B.E.A.M.A. " A " conditions:

You [*i.e.* the buyer] assume responsibility that goods stipulated by you are sufficient and suitable for your purpose save in so far as your stipulations are in accordance with our [*i.e.* the seller's] advice.

The intention of this is to ensure that the seller, in this case the manufacturer of the goods, will not be held to be liable under the implied condition of section 14 (1) unless he has expressly in his tender stated that the goods are suited to the purpose disclosed by the purchaser. Thus, whilst the Act causes the condition to be applied if:
   (a) the purpose is disclosed,
   (b) the buyer shows that he relies upon the seller's skill and judgment,
   (c) the goods are of a description which it is in the business of the seller to supply,
to this the words quoted add a fourth qualification, namely that the seller has expressly advised in the matter.

Here again, the Misrepresentation Act 1967 can limit the success of this attempt. If, in pre-contract negotiations, the seller has declared that the goods are suitable for the purpose disclosed, this will constitute a representation, and if it subsequently transpires that they were not suitable, it will be shown to have been a misrepresentation. An attempt to escape from liability on the ground that the misrepresentation was not contained in the tender document itself is likely to fail by virtue of section 3 of the Misrepresentation Act.

When the conditions put forward by buyers are examined, it will be observed that the tendency is the other way. The **Purchasing Officers' Association** provide that the goods ordered shall " if the purpose for which they are required is indicated in the Order, whether expressly or by implication, be fit for that purpose." Thus, whilst the seller *adds* a condition for the implication of the conditions to be effective, the buyer eliminates (b) and (c) of those quoted above. As has been mentioned, the Purchasing Officers' Association's conditions are moderate, and if any complaint by manufacturers is justified, it is not that they are unreasonable but that they are not used. Individual buyers tend to write their own purchase conditions. Thus, one example runs:

> Vendor warrants that all articles furnished hereunder are free from any defects . . . and fully comply with specifications and when not specified the articles are suitable and fit for the use intended. The articles covered by this purchase order are purchased from the Vendor in reliance upon the aforementioned Warranty of Vendor.

In this case the vendor is apparently assumed to know for what purpose the goods are being acquired, whether the order discloses this or not, but reasonably, the purchaser does not require him to take any responsibility for the suitability of goods for which the purchaser has given a specification.

More exacting and typical of the emphasis placed by buyers on this principle is the following:

> The Purchaser relies upon the skill and judgment of the Supplier and the Supplier shall include in its price for and forthwith advise the Purchaser in writing of any alterations which may be necessary to ensure that the resulting products are fit for the purposes and capable of the performance specified by the Purchaser. Subject as aforesaid, the Supplier shall strictly comply with all such Specifications, Designs, Drawings, Samples and Descriptions and with all such instructions and guarantees that the resulting product will be fit for the purposes and capable of the performances specified by the Purchaser.

Upon analysis it is likely to be felt that such a clause goes farther than is reasonable. It is put forward by a firm of specialist engineers whom one would have thought to have themselves been the best judges of the goods which would be needed for their special purposes, so that if they produce a detailed specification for a material or machine it is hardly justifiable that they should expect their supplier to judge whether their specification is properly prepared and to suggest alterations if it is not. Between the B.E.A.M.A. clause already quoted and this there is a complete contradiction. The sponsor of this last clause is a company which buys extensively from members of the electrical industry who habitually sell subject to B.E.A.M.A. conditions, and one wonders how often the conflict is brought into the light of day.

(iii) *Performance*

Statements made regarding the performance of machinery and their recognition as conditions of the contract of sale constitute a special case under the general subject of sale of goods by description. It is clear that apart from any express qualification in the contract documents a representation made by the seller upon the basis of which the buyer has entered into contract will be a condition of the sale, so that failure of the machine to perform as promised will prima facie provide grounds for an action on the part of the buyer. Because this is so, the customary approach of the seller is by his conditions to exclude all such statements from the contract unless at the time of tendering he has repeated them in the most express form. Thus B.E.A.M.A. " A " conditions state:

> We will accept no liability for failure to attain any performance figures quoted by us unless we have specifically guaranteed them subject to any tolerances specified or agreed by us, in an agreed sum as liquidated damages.

In the interpretation of a clause of this kind it is necessary to have regard to the general principles of contract and to the possibility of conflict between printed conditions and what has been written in the contract documents.[4] It is possible to place more reliance upon such a clause as this than is justified. It is, however, evidence of the attempt of the seller to limit the contractual effect of any representations he may have made either expressly in relation to the goods which are the subject of the contract, or in a more general way by means of his published material.

Naturally, the purchaser seeks to place reliance on the wording of his order. The Purchasing Officers Association's conditions

---

4 See section below, " The application of conditions of sale," p. 40.

provide that the goods shall " be capable of any standard of performance specified in the order," but in making this stipulation the conditions do not exclude the possibility of relying upon any representation made by the seller on the basis of which the contract may have been placed.

In the sale and purchase of machinery both seller and buyer are well advised to study the provisions of the contract critically, because disputes concerning performance are easily engendered and are difficult to settle. It should be recognised that representations or guarantees of performance fall into two very different categories. The first kind of performance guarantee is a representation regarding the inherent quality of the machine. Thus the efficiency of an electric motor is a function of its mechanical and electric design, and it is to this type of performance figures that the qualified provision of the B.E.A.M.A. conditions applies. The second kind of representation is that which relates to the actual quantity or quality of work which the machine will do in operation, in the case especially of production machinery, its output measured in tons or feet or gallons. The attainment of any such standard is bound to be dependent upon the quality of the raw material used and the skill which is displayed in the operation of the machine. For this reason the manufacturers of specialised production machinery should be particularly cautious in offering such guarantees.

It is sometimes represented that a machine shall be " capable of " a specified performance or output. Unless the parties are clear at the outset as to the meaning of the phrase they may be storing up trouble for themselves. Whether a machine is capable of a specified performance is in the last degree a question of fact, but a fact which it is by no means easy to establish. It may be capable of the represented performance only if operated with the best quality of material and the highest degree of skill, and fail lamentably when the buyer attempts to work the machine using inferior material or placing it under the control of an inexperienced operator. One method which is used in the attempt to clarify the obligations of the parties in such a situation is to provide that if the buyer, within a stated period, alleges that the machine has failed to live up to its manufacturer's promises, the manufacturer shall have the opportunity of operating the machine by his own team in the buyer's works to show that it can perform as promised.

If he succeeds the cost of the operation will fall on the seller, who, of course, will benefit by the educative value of the demonstration. It is well to have some provision written into the contract to show what is to happen if he fails. Without such provision there will have been a fundamental failure on the part of the seller to provide what was bargained for, and the buyer could legally reject the goods and sue for damages. Some formula of price modification related to the true capacity of the machine will be more likely to meet the convenience of both parties.

(iv) *Time for delivery*

At no point is there more difference between the attitude of buyer and seller in the wording of the conditions that are to apply to a contract for the sale of goods than in the clause or clauses relating to the time for the goods to be made available to the buyer.

It is well to examine the position on the basis of the general law of contract and the Sale of Goods Act, which in section 10 (1) states:

> Unless a different intention appears from the terms of the contract stipulations as to time of payment are not deemed to be of the essence of the contract. *Whether any other stipulation as to time is of the essence of the contract or not depends upon the terms of the contract.*

This appears to leave wide open the question whether times appointed for delivery are of the essence of the contract of sale. The trend of the cases, however, has been such as to remove any doubt that might have been felt, and it is clear that in the absence of an express or implied intention to the contrary failure to deliver goods in accordance with the contract at the time stipulated in the contract is a fundamental breach giving rise not only to damages on the part of the aggrieved buyer but also entitling him to treat the contract as breached, and, if he wishes, to buy elsewhere or refuse to accept the goods altogether. Further, the defaulting seller may be liable in consequential damages.

Whereas the ruling cases on this matter are fairly old, this last point was illustrated in a case [5] sufficiently recent as to have been considered by the courts against a background that would

5 *Victoria Laundry (Windsor) Ltd.* v. *Newman Industries Coulson & Co. (Third Parties)* [1949] 2 K.B. 528.

have given prominence to the technical problem attending modern industry and would have provided a good deal in the way of extenuating circumstances to the defaulter, yet the decision went against him, and it stands as a warning to any seller of technical products to exercise care in the wording of his contracts. In this case the defendants contracted to sell a second-hand boiler to the plaintiffs, to deliver it on a stated date, and to " put it into use in the shortest possible space of time." Between the date of making the contract and the date for delivery of the boiler, third parties, engaged to dismantle the boiler preparatory to its conveyance to the plaintiff's laundry, caused damage to it so that it could not be effectively delivered and put to work until about five months later. The court decided not only that there was an actionable breach of contract on the part of the vendors, but also that the plaintiffs were entitled to claim as damages a reasonable estimate of such of the profits lost to them by reason of the delay in the expansion of their business, to achieve which they had purchased the boiler, as could reasonably have been foreseen by the defendants.

It is clear that this situation is one which sellers will seek to avoid, whilst buyers will be in a position of advantage in so far as it can be maintained. The B.E.A.M.A. clause accordingly provides:

> *Liability for delay.* Any times quoted for despatch or delivery are to date from receipt by us of a written order to proceed and of all necessary information and drawings to enable us to put the work in hand. The time for despatch or delivery shall be extended by a reasonable period if delay in despatch or delivery is caused by instructions or lack of instructions from you or by industrial dispute or by any cause beyond our reasonable control.
>
> If a fixed time be quoted for despatch or delivery, and we fail to despatch or deliver within that time or within any extension thereof provided by this clause, and if as a result you shall have suffered loss, we undertake to pay for each week or part of a week of delay, liquidated damages at the rate of — per cent. up to a maximum of — per cent. of that portion of the price named in the contract which is referable to such portion only of the contract goods as cannot in

consequence of the delay be used commercially and effectively. Such payment shall be in full satisfaction of our liability for delay.

Any time described as an estimate shall not be construed as a fixed time quoted for the purpose of this clause.

It will be observed that if this clause had been written into the contract, the seller who has failed to deliver at the proper time is in a very strong position. He has four possible lines of retreat.

(a) He can argue that the buyer has not in fact suffered loss.

(b) He can claim an extension of time on the basis of alleged circumstances outside his control.

(c) He can only be made liable if he has expressly agreed to be liable for delay in " liquidated damages," which then operates as a limit.

(d) Even liquidated damages [6] can only be claimed by the aggrieved buyer if he has in fact suffered loss.

Further, if the blank spaces in the clause were not completed, as would frequently happen, there would be no liability.

The buyer, on the other hand, always seeks to maintain the common law position. The moderate Purchasing Officers' Association conditions provide that " The Seller shall deliver the Goods at the time specified in the Order." They give to the seller the right to claim an extension of time in the event of delay being caused by circumstances outside his control, and provide that the seller shall be granted such extension of time as may be reasonable. The buyer is then given the right in the event of default (after allowing for any extension granted) to cancel the contract in respect of the undelivered goods and to claim as damages the expense of obtaining other goods in replacement. These conditions do not expressly provide for any claim for consequential damages by the aggrieved buyer, but neither do they exclude such a claim. Unless such an exclusion could be inferred from the surrounding circumstances, the custom of a trade or the course of dealing, the liability to consequential damages would therefore appear to remain.

While these conditions are buyer-orientated they are not, however, presented as " buyer's conditions." " They have been

---

[6] See below, p. 95.

drawn up," says the Association, "with the object of being fair and reasonable to both parties," and notwithstanding the findings in the case referred to on p. 23, the Association advises buyers that the right to buy elsewhere and charge the seller with the extra cost is inappropriate where the goods bought consist of "capital plant or tailormade items" and "the Buyer will have to be content with liquidated damages for delay."

Perhaps the very moderation of these professionally sponsored conditions is the cause for their relatively infrequent use. Buyers who feel themselves to be in a position to call the tune take a very different line. Thus the standard conditions of purchase of the National Coal Board state boldly:

> The goods . . . shall be delivered by the Seller at the time or times . . . specified in the order and performance of this condition shall be of the essence of the contract.

Another set of buyers' conditions:

> The date for commencement of delivery and the rate and period of delivery specified in this Order shall be strictly adhered to by the Seller and we reserve the right to cancel any contract based upon this Order either wholly or as regards any balance of it without redress if not executed within the time specified and to debit the Seller with any loss which we incur thereby or resulting from our having to resort to alternative sources of supply.

The gulf between the typical attitude of seller and buyer in this matter of time of delivery is so complete that it is interesting to compare the professionally sponsored I.Mech.E./I.E.E. conditions. The lengthy clause 7 deals with the subject, and represents, as would be anticipated, a middle position. The seller is entitled to claim an extension of time in the event of delay for reasons beyond his control, but subject to this he is entitled to treat his quoted times as estimates only if he has described them so. If he defaults he is liable in liquidated damages, but then only if the buyer has in fact suffered loss. By the provision of sub-paragraph (v) consequential damages are excluded, but the buyer has the right to cancel the contract in the event of default, if this is extended and warning has been given.

It is perhaps desirable to comment upon the use of the word

" consequential " in connection with damages. It is often bandied about as though it had a clearly understood meaning, but it is not, in fact, a " term of art " – as the lawyer would say. The legal theory of the assessment of damages is set out clearly by the judgment in the classic case *Hadley* v. *Baxendale* (1854) 9 Ex. 341, p. 355, quoted in most books on the law of contract. In it the quantum of damages is the measure of injury which the aggrieved party has suffered provided it could be considered as either (a) arising naturally according to the ordinary course of things and within the contemplation of the parties at the time of making the contract, or (b) being the probable result of special circumstances communicated to the defaulting party at the time when the contract was made. What is excluded from this definition is injury resulting from special circumstances unknown to the defaulting party or not existing or reasonably foreseeable when the contract was made. Within this analysis there is no distinction between damages which are or are not " consequential." The term is used among business people to indicate that kind of injury to one's interests which is relatively remote and not capable of being clearly envisaged by the party in default when the contract was made. Since no loss or injury can rank for damages at all unless it is the *consequence* of the default, all damages are necessarily " consequential."

There is little doubt that the most intractable problem in the attempt to create completely fair and workable conditions to operate between the buyer and seller of goods is this one of the sanction to be applied in the event of late delivery, and consequently the means available to the buyer to ensure that he obtains his goods at the time he needs them. It has been seen that the typical conditions extant fall into three groups. Sellers' conditions seek to avoid liability, buyers' to fix full responsibility, including consequential damages, and more moderate conditions provide for liquidated damages. In modern industry the problem of late dispatch is a serious one, and in the opinion of many observers failure to keep quoted dispatch times is the prime sin of modern industry. There are both reasons and excuses for lateness, however, and the problem is not as easy in practice as it appears to the lawyers in the uncomplicated atmosphere of a court. It may therefore be of value to stand back from this problem and, forgetting the wording of rival conditions, attempt to see it whole and objectively. Upon almost every other point in the cleavage of interest between buyer and seller a compromise can readily be found by negotiation. Upon this, however, the difference of approach between the two parties is so fundamental that the unsatisfactory compromise of " liquidated damages " is very frequently adopted simply because it is difficult to find a better.

It is unsatisfactory for a number of reasons. The very fact that the adverse consequences to the seller of defaulting in the matter of time can be measured with accuracy may constitute a temptation to allow in his costing for a measure of " penalty " to be applied, and then to hope for the best. If pressures develop which give rise to a general deterioration in the delivery position the manufacturer will naturally balance penalty against penalty and bias his production plans so as to operate to his least disadvantage in this respect, rather than consider the extent to which his customers will in fact be damaged by his default. The reduction in price which the application of " liquidated damages " affords to the buyer seldom matches the damage actually suffered. Sometimes the buyer who is kept waiting for his goods loses nothing thereby, but if he suffers at all his loss is likely to exceed anything he may receive as liquidated damages. Thus the device fails in its ostensible purpose, in that it is seldom a genuine pre-estimate of the damage that will be suffered by the buyer. It is normally qualified by a provision under which the seller is entitled to call for an extension of time if delay is due to circumstances over which he has no control, and it is so easy for the seller to make such a claim with his full knowledge of the circumstances and to find plausible excuses, and so difficult for the buyer to refute it, that in practice it is found that to invoke the liquidated damages clause is to invite vexatious argument and to generate ill-will.

In this book the attempt throughout is to concentrate upon typical situations, and the typical situation in which the maintenance of delivery promises is of vital importance is that in which the goods to be supplied are made specially for the customer, and are such that their manufacture is a relatively lengthy process. In other situations the problem is not acute. If goods of like kind can be readily purchased elsewhere the buyer can help himself out of the difficulty by buying in the market, and the seller who is left with goods on his hands can similarly sell them on the market.

The damage which either suffers if there is a breach of contract is easily measurable as the difference in price, and the situation is adequately dealt with in the Sale of Goods Act, which, as has already been observed, grew out of the decisions of the courts made over a period when the contract of sale was mostly a matter for merchants dealing with commodities. When, however, an order is placed for goods which are specially made, the buyer has placed himself in the hands of the seller in a quite different way. Probably only those concerned in manufacturing industry can have a proper sense of the problems that arise when default occurs, or properly assess the difficulties that may be the cause of default. It is by no means unusual for the construction of a complicated machine, or, indeed, for a relatively standard article, if it is large and made only to order, to occupy a year of factory time. It is easy for the law to apply principles, valid enough in their proper place, granting the aggrieved buyer the right to repudiate the contract breached by the defaulting seller and to buy the goods elsewhere, but in practice that is the last thing he is likely to do, because to do it is to sacrifice such progress as has been made in the factory, and to recommence, with a new manufacturer, the long waiting period required for design and the organisation of manufacture. If he does cancel the contract the true reason may be that he has changed his plans and is using the opportunity thus gratuitously offered to escape from his commitments. Looking at the same situation from the point of view of the seller, it is equally easy for the law to say that he has defaulted and has failed to deliver the goods at the proper time so that the buyer is released from the contract and that he, as the seller, has only himself to blame. But to be left with a nearly completed machine for which there is no immediate prospect of sale and which represents the investment of many thousands of pounds in production costs is a major catastrophe which he cannot contemplate with any equanimity. Thus, once an order for this type of article is placed, the two parties are deeply committed to each other by the practical realities of the situation.

From the point of view of the buyer, however, the availability of the goods at the time contracted for may be absolutely vital. He may himself have entered into commitments upon the strength of the seller's undertakings. When the goods are themselves to be used for production purposes as earning assets, delay may

involve him in trading losses and in breach of his own undertakings. Of what value to him is a liquidated damages clause
yielding a maximum of £1,000, if, as a result of the delay he
loses profits worth ten times as much, involves himself in lawsuits
from the breach of his own contracts, and suffers a loss of
reputation which cannot be appraised? For him, the best position
is to be able to recognise time as of the essence of the contract,
and to rest upon the common law principle expressed in the Sale
of Goods Act, " The measure of damages is the estimated loss
directly and naturally resulting in the ordinary course of events
from the seller's breach of contract." As has been seen, the
damages recoverable at common law by the application of this
principle can be very heavy and can include loss of profits.

But the seller also has his point of view. When he quotes a
time for the supply of the goods he is looking into the future,
which is always a risky business. It is not merely a matter of
fire, flood, act of God, industrial dispute, embargo, riot, or any
other hair-raising possibilities which legal draftsmen love to write
into their escape clauses. His chief designer may fall sick, or
find another job, or a flaw may be found in a major casting, so
that it has to be replaced from the foundry, or he may be kept
waiting for components he has ordered from other suppliers. He
may find it difficult to work to required tolerances without seeking
new standards of material. It may simply happen that a job
takes longer than he had expected, or that a sub-assembly has to
be redesigned because of teething troubles. Just how far can he
expect to stretch an escape clause based upon the magical words
" circumstances beyond his reasonable control " ? The two things
he dare not expose himself to are to have his custom built machine
left on his hands and to be held liable to damages when he has
genuinely done his best to fulfil his promises.

Now practical men can see these two points of view. Buyers
are not, as human beings, unreasonable, nor are sellers. There
is, none the less, real importance in the principle that promises
are made to be kept, and that the seller who breaks his promises
should be held responsible. The truth is that the practice which
buyers wish to be armed against is the tendency of sellers to
quote delivery times frivolously or recklessly or fraudulently.
This last is a strong word to use, but one that is sometimes
justified. It is very frequently the case that the time quoted for

delivery is of more significance in the award of a competitive tender than is the price quoted. If the earning power of a production machine is £2,000 per month it is better to buy it for £10,000 and have it in six months than to pay £8,000 and to wait for a year. It is plainly fraudulent for a manufacturer in order to obtain business against honest competitors who have quoted realistically, to add ten per cent. to his proper price and state a delivery date which he well knows is impossible of achievement, offering a liquidated damages clause which at the maximum will absorb the loading he has injected into his price. It is fraudulent, but that is not to say that it has never been done.

What are the possible sanctions for non-delivery at the promised time, and when, in fairness, ought they to be applied? It is suggested that the reasonable answers are as follows:

(a) The right of the buyer to cancel the contract and to buy elsewhere. This, as has been shown, is often impracticable, and operates unjustly against the seller who has made a reasonable effort to fulfil his obligations, but has met with unexpected difficulties, even though those difficulties do not come within the usually accepted meaning of *force majeure*. It is, however, a sanction which should be available as a last resort to relieve the buyer from a contract in the event of complete incompetence on the part of the seller.

(b) The right on the part of the buyer to claim damages at large, which can include loss of profits provided they are reasonably foreseeable. This operates excessively harshly against an honest seller who has met with unexpected difficulties, but is fully justifiable against a seller who has quoted recklessly or fraudulently in the matter of delivery time.

(c) Liquidated damages, usually subject to an escape clause dealing with the more obvious kinds of *force majeure*. This is unlikely to recompense the aggrieved buyer adequately, but provides an incentive to a seller to do his utmost to minimise delays which occur in respect of promises made in good faith, but arise in the course of manufacture when there has been some lack of alertness on the part of the manufacturer.

It is submitted that, having regard to the realities of present-day business, the proper aim in framing the contract of sale in such cases is to cause the manufacturer who has quoted an early delivery recklessly or fraudulently to bear the full rigour of the common law remedy, to ensure a proper liaison between buyer and seller at all stages of production, so that the buyer is kept aware of any delays which are occurring, and, at the same time, whilst not bearing harshly upon the honest supplier who has met with unexpected difficulties, not to allow him to go completely unscathed for his lack of proper attention and foresight. The sanction should therefore be, in summary form:

    (a) In the event of lateness being attributed to irresponsible quotation in the first place, the full sanction available under the common law.

    (b) In the event of lateness being attributable to unforeseen difficulties or delays arising within the normal operation of the business, *i.e.* not due to *force majeure,* a moderate measure of liquidated damages, subject to a maximum.

    (c) In the event of lateness being due to *force majeure, i.e.* supervening circumstances quite outside the control of the supplier and not to be foreseen by him, no adverse consequences, provided he has kept the buyer advised.

To frame a clause which would have this effect is necessarily to perpetrate a complicated piece of drafting, and to introduce some provision for the arbitrator to decide the necessarily subjective question of the state of mind of the defaulter, but the following is offered as a suggestion.

    (a) The date fixed for the completion of the contract is — which date is accepted by both parties as reasonable and practicable. The buyer declares that in the event of delay beyond that date he is liable to suffer damage and, subject as hereinafter provided, reserves the right to claim damages at large in the event of default by the seller. The seller declares that the said date is based upon his reasonable expectations at the date of entering into the contract and acknowledges that he shall forfeit his right to the benefit of the next sub-clause if it shall be shown that such date was not quoted in good faith.

(b) The seller shall advise the buyer in the event of any circumstances arising or becoming evident which shall cause completion of the contract to be delayed. Provided such circumstances are such as could not reasonably be foreseen at the time of entering into the contract, the said date shall be extended by such period as shall be reasonably necessary, but unless the delay shall be due to *force majeure* as hereinafter defined, this shall be without prejudice to the buyer receiving by way of liquidated damages and not as penalty in full satisfaction a reduction of the contract price at the rate of — per cent. for every week of delay after the first — weeks provided that the maximum such deduction shall be — per cent.

(c) If any delay (whether or not coming under the provisions of the last sub-clause) shall exceed — weeks then the buyer shall be entitled to give notice in writing to the seller that if the seller shall not have fulfilled the contract within a further — weeks the buyer shall be entitled to treat the contract as having been terminated.

(d) *Force majeure* shall mean fire, flood, tempest, industrial dispute [. . . the list can be suited to the industry concerned . . .] but shall not include unforeseen difficulties in manufacture, difficulty in obtaining supplies (unless itself due to *force majeure*), shortage of labour or other causes arising within the seller's establishment.

(e) Any dispute arising under this clause including a dispute as to whether the said date was quoted in good faith shall be referred to the arbitration of a single arbitrator agreed by the parties or in default of agreement appointed by . . . and such reference shall be deemed to be a submission to arbitration under the Arbitration Act 1950.

Such a clause supposes that the parties will have confidence both in the fairmindedness and the ability of the arbitrator, who would need to be a person with considerable knowledge of the industry concerned. It is designed, in addition to making a distinction between irresponsibility and misfortune, to surround

D

with some solemnity the quotation of the date for completion, in the belief that this in itself would go a long way towards discouraging a casual or irresponsible attitude towards delivery promises, which, in the opinion of many people, is the besetting sin of latter-day business practice.

(v) *Defects and maintenance guarantees*

The common law and the Sale of Goods Act make no provision for the acceptance of any obligations by the seller of goods under which he assumes any responsibility to effect repairs without charge for a limited period after sale. This very general practice is entirely the creation of written contracts, for the most part enshrined in " Conditions of Sale " and for the better edification of the buyer in the retail trade, frequently evidenced by flamboyant and pretentious documents.

This does not, of course, mean that the common law and the Act left a buyer without a remedy if he had been sold goods which at the time of sale were actually defective in a way that could not be detected by inspection. He would be protected by the implied condition of merchantable quality and, if the circumstances were such as to cause it to apply, suitability for the purpose for which the goods were acquired. Clearly, a motor car that will not start is not of merchantable quality. Almost as clearly one that breaks down within the first ten miles could not have been of merchantable quality at the time of sale, although the fault might not have been discernible to normal inspection. As the time between sale and the discovery of a defect lengthens the difficulty of deciding whether goods were defective at the time of the sale increases, and the now traditional practice of giving a maintenance guarantee limited in time has grown naturally out of the increasing importance of technical products in the markets of the world.

The purpose of these clauses can be viewed as being made up of three elements. The first is a common acceptance of the principle that the manufacturer of goods, especially of a technical nature, should be responsible for ensuring that they operate properly when installed in the ownership of the buyer. Whether this responsibility could be read in the common law principles is a moot point depending upon the question how much can be read into the phrase " merchantable quality," but as a principle it is now commercially accepted without dispute.   The second element may be regarded as the value of the clause to the seller in setting clearly defined limits to his liability and in being the vehicle whereby he excludes liabilities that would otherwise fall upon him.   The third element is the value of the clause to the buyer in enabling him to extract as much as possible in the way of after sales service from the seller.

The B.E.A.M.A. standard guarantee is typical of many and is an interesting example of the frank acceptance of a continuing responsibility for twelve months, coupled with a determination to protect the manufacturer by limitations and exclusions:

> We will make good by repair or at our option by the supply of a replacement defects which under proper use appear in the goods *within a period of twelve calendar months* after the goods have been delivered and arise *solely* from faulty design, materials or workmanship: provided always that defective parts are *promptly returned by you free to our works* unless otherwise arranged . . . *and our liability under this clause shall be in lieu of any warranty or condition implied by law as to the quality or fitness for any particular purpose of such goods.*

It is arguable that this clause as worded concedes nothing that would not, in its absence, be an obligation of the seller under common law and the Sale of Goods Act, whilst it excludes some liabilities that in its absence would exist.   The words italicised all operate as limitations or exclusions.   It is fair to state that for the most part the hundreds of manufacturers who use this clause operate it generously and do not apply the limitations narrowly. It is, however, a careful piece of drafting in the interest of the manufacturer.

Buyers tend to be more exacting.   The Purchasing Officers' Association conditions require that:

> The Seller shall with all possible speed replace or repair the goods so as to remedy the defects without cost to the Buyer.

A typical clause indorsed on an order form reads as follows:

> Any defects not disclosed prior to acceptance of materials by Purchaser which shall develop within one year after commencement of operation or within fifteen months from

the date of dispatch whichever is shorter shall be promptly remedied by Vendor free of charge to Purchaser and all expense of transportation for such repairs or replacement shall be borne by Vendor.

An illustration of the practical difference arising as between typical sellers' and buyers' conditions each based upon what would popularly be called " twelve months maintenance guarantee " may be seen by comparing the B.E.A.M.A. clause already quoted with the clause used in a set of conditions used by British Rail in respect of locomotives.   This reads as follows:

> For a period of twelve months after the plant has been taken over . . . the contractor shall be responsible for any defects arising from faulty materials or workmanship in the plant and shall forthwith at his own expense remedy such defects as called upon to do so by the engineer who shall state in writing in what respect any portion is faulty.

If the defect became evident by an electrical breakdown immobilising the locomotive in a distant location, under the B.E.A.M.A. conditions the cost of towing it back to workshop, dismantling the machinery, isolating the defective component, sending it to its manufacturer and subsequently installing the repaired component or its replacement would fall upon the buyer.   Under the Rail conditions these costs could fall on the seller.   They could in the aggregate far exceed the cost of the actual repair.

A not uncommon refinement of this type of clause when put forward by a buyer is that when under guarantee goods or parts thereof are repaired or renewed the repaired or renewed parts shall be held under guarantee for a period (generally identical with the normal guarantee period) calculated from the date of renewal or repair.

(vi) *The right of cancellation*

Legally, a contract once made is binding and the intending buyer who changes his mind has no right to cancel his order. The position was exhaustively examined in a case [7] that went to

---

[7] *White and Carter (Councils) Ltd.* v. *McGregor* [1962] A.C. 413.   This was a Scottish case.   The decision of the House of Lords was by majority and the dissenting judgments of Lords Keith and Morton supported the contrary

the House of Lords. The plaintiff held a concession from a local authority to affix advertising plaques to litter bins supplied by him to the local authority. The defendant, by one of its employees, placed an order with the plaintiff for the manufacture of a quantity of these advertisements. Before any work had been done by the plaintiff in the execution of the order the defendant sought to countermand the instructions of his employee and to cancel the order. It was held not merely that the plaintiff was entitled to claim damages, but that he was entitled to ignore the purported cancellation, proceed with the order and charge in full.

It must be admitted that, in general, the practice of commerce and industry is less intransigent, and it is customary for a manu-facturing seller to accept cancellation of an order at the request of the intended buyer upon payment of what is usually called a cancellation charge, but which is in truth a sum constituting agreed damages for the breach of contract of the buyer. When no work has been done at the date of cancellation the charge may be waived altogether, limited to a nominal sum or be so fixed as to represent only the anticipated profit on the cancelled work. As the quantity of work done increases, so the cancellation charge increases steeply.

The law being as it is, it is against the interest of the seller to include any provisions in his conditions to deal with the contin-gency. The buyer wishing to cancel is then very much in the hands of the seller and has little option but to pay the charge imposed. In buyers' conditions, however, the provision for cancellation of an order is frequently included. The Purchasing Officers' Association make no such provision, however. The most detailed treatment contained in standard conditions is perhaps that provided by the Standard Conditions of Government Con-tracts for Stores Purchases originated by the former Ministry of Supply and now used widely by government departments with slight amendments. The clause, known as the " Break Clause," is one of the optional clauses, that is to say, it does not apply unless expressly included when a contract is made. Its effect is to give the purchasing authority the right to cancel the contract

---

argument that the seller was under obligation to mitigate his loss and to claim only the sum remaining as loss after such mitigation. In the circum-stances of this case this could have been at the most, only the anticipated profit on the deal.

at any time by due notice and it defines in considerable detail the compensation to which the supplier is to be entitled. It provides for the supplier, if so required, to cease production and determine sub-contracts on the best terms possible, for the authority to take over all completed or partly completed work or bought-out components at a valuation and to require the contractor to dispose of any unused material as directed. The contractor is indemnified against commitments and expenditures he has properly entered into and is entitled to claim a discretionary allowance if the cancellation causes hardship.

This clause is one that makes very much more effort to be just than some which are included by individual buyers. Thus, one set of purchasing conditions contains the following:

> We shall be entitled at any time by fourteen days' notice in writing to determine the contract and on such determination:
>
> (a) The Seller shall assign to us if it is practicable to do so the benefit of any subcontract entered into by the Seller in connection with the goods the subject of this order or terminate any such sub-contract.
>
> (b) The Seller shall be entitled to be paid;
>
> > (i) the sums remaining payable to the Seller under the terms of this order in respect of work done and goods provided up to the date of termination,
> >
> > (ii) any sums which have necessarily been paid by the Seller in order to carry out the Seller's obligations under (a) above,
> >
> > (iii) any other reasonable costs or expenses incurred by the Seller by reason of such determination.
>
> The Seller will not be entitled to any further payment. Should any dispute arise . . . [here follows a procedure for arbitration].

More peremptory still is the following:

> We shall be entitled to cancel in whole or in part any contract based on this order . . . at any time and for any reason. In such event our liability . . . shall be confined to the amount of the Seller's costs and commitments properly incurred in relation to the cancelled portion of such contract (after making due allowance for salvage value) taking no

account of consequential loss or of any loss of materials or work procured or carried out before the time which would normally be required to enable the Seller to meet the specified delivery date or dates.

It does not require any deep knowledge of manufacturing processes and the organisation of business to discern that such a clause provides inadequate compensation for the loss and dislocation caused by the unexpected cancellation of a large order in process of manufacture.

In fact, none of the three clauses quoted, not even that from the Government conditions, is such as to give the manufacturing supplier a fair settlement, and the fact that sellers are better served by not having such a clause at all has prevented the emergence of any generally agreed norm. The rigour of the common law situation as already described is unreasonably harsh to a buyer who for sufficient reason finds it necessary or desirable to cancel an order. But a reasonable compensation to the seller in such circumstances would be more generous than that which is written into these clauses. It should take into account not only the expenditure which he has actually incurred but also the consequences of dislocation resulting from the rearrangement of manufacturing programmes, and should make some allowance also for the loss of anticipated profits.

(vii) *Miscellaneous matters*

The foregoing illustrate the principal directions in which buyers and sellers seek to supplement or to modify the terms of contract that would operate if the Sale of Goods Act alone provided the rules to govern it. In addition each trade tends to have its special type of provision, and the special circumstances of sub-contracting, or of placing with outside manufacturers the manufacture of sub-assemblies or components introduce special terms into the contract of sale. These special cases operate, however, less as modifications of the basic provisions of the Sale of Goods Act than as the filling in of detail where this is necessary.

In this category are clauses dealing with the ownership and use of patterns and moulds or the use of specially made jigs, dies and tools. Similarly, in the case of specially made small articles. it is usual to provide for a tolerance in the number to be supplied, so that a marginal overrun or underrun on production does not constitute a breach of contract.

An interesting clause is that dealing with secrecy. The placing of orders, especially with sub-contractors and component manufacturers, may require the release of information which, in the wrong hands, could be used to the buyer's detriment. He will frequently seek to avoid this by writing into his purchase conditions provisions having the effect of precluding the use of information except for the execution of the order. How effective such provisions are in practice is a matter of conjecture. How far they are legally enforceable is a question for a specialist. Their principal shortcoming is that, if binding at all, they bind only the seller and not his individual employees, and it is the individual employee who would be most likely to be responsible for any breach of secrecy.

It is usual for the buyer to retain copyright in drawings and to require the return of the originals and of any copies, where questions of trade secrets are thought likely to arise. Sometimes the form taken is to restrain the seller from manufacturing machinery incorporating any design feature contained in the buyer's designs for a stated period. The difficulty with any such clause is that of saying whether, at some time in the future, a new machine does or does not incorporate such a feature. Strictly speaking, there is no enforceable proprietary right in ideas as such, and the law regarding patents and registered designs is directed to giving the protection which the law regards as reasonable in respect of this type of industrial property; if the purchaser wants protection for his ideas he should seek it through this branch of the law. The nature of the contract of sale, however, is that such a clause is enforceable in so far as it can be made sufficiently certain in interpretation and is not in unreasonable restraint of trade. Its acceptance by the seller remains a matter of commercial expediency.

3. The application of conditions of sale

It is one thing to provide for a set of conditions and to hope that they will apply to a contract for the sale or purchase of goods, it is another to be sure that they will in fact apply. Many undertakings which are equipped with comprehensive conditions for the transactions normally carried out by them are found to exercise little or no care to ensure that those conditions do apply. Indeed, it would be difficult to see how it can be done under present conditions unless the undertaking concerned is the dominant party in the contract (either as buyer or seller) and unless the type of business is such that the number of individual contracts is small enough to bring each under competent scrutiny. In the normal transactions of a buying office or of a department receiving orders in the offices of a wholesaler or manufacturer the most that can be done is to exercise a general supervision so that the more objectionable clauses (according to whether one is buying or selling) are discerned and either rejected or modified. How true this is can be seen by the course of events in the engineering industries since, say, 1945. Then, at the end of the war the demand for engineering products was so great that the seller was dominant. Organised into trade associations matched to the broad sections of the industry sellers tended to impose standard conditions of sale and were able to insist upon their acceptance. They were able, for example, to insist upon the acceptance of the so-called " p.r.d." (price ruling at date of dispatch) clause by which the buyer undertook to pay for the goods at whatever price was " ruling " (which meant little more precise than that which the seller imposed) at a date which might be two or more years ahead. Gradually the larger buyers whose business was important to the manufacturers were able to insist upon modifications, and exceptions began to be made to the rigid rules. After some years the manufacturer ceased to be in a position to dictate: he could no longer feel that there would be six new purchasers clamouring for his products if one buyer turned away. Competition began to be felt among the manufacturers themselves, and those who needed orders proved compliant in the matter of conditions. The trade associations no longer disciplined their members in the matter of conditions and merely " recommended." At length the Restrictive Trade Practices Act 1956 administered the *coup de grâce* to the practices by which the trade associations were able, besides fixing level prices, to impose standard conditions, and the advantages of economic strength tended to pass to the buyer. Every purchasing officer began to think of the exploitation of his new-found strength, shaping the contract to his own advantage, and a variety of buyer-drafted conditions began to be endorsed on inquiry and order forms, more outrageous in their demands than the old sellers' conditions ever were. Amongst other things the old p.r.d. clauses, and even clauses providing for price variation by formula became almost unknown in sectors of industry where they had been usual, and it is common knowledge that in consequence the inflationary pressures of the years from 1969 onward caused some undertakings to become involved in very serious losses.

As a result of the present situation it is often difficult or impossible to spell out a contract from the documents, since each party has purported to contract on a set of conditions which the other has ignored or rejected. It will often be found upon close analysis that there is, in the last resort, no contract. Advocating the suggestion that the legislature should itself impose standard conditions for certain typical contracts, the author of an article some years ago claimed as an advantage that " far less time would be wasted in solicitor's offices, barrister's chambers and the courts in trying to find out which documents, if any, formed part of the contract, and how they could be read together, if at all." [8]

In interpreting such a situation it is necessary to go back to first principles. For a contract to exist it is necessary for the two parties to be *ad idem*. The law always seeks to analyse a contract into an offer and an acceptance. If a supposed acceptance of an offer purports to vary any of the terms of the offer it is not legally an acceptance: it is a counter-offer. If the other party treats it as an acceptance and by his conduct shows that he is willing to proceed upon the new terms, his conduct may amount to a tacit or implied acceptance of the counter-offer. *At some point,* if there is to be a contract at all, it must be possible to show that all the terms comprised on the final offer or counter-offer have been accepted by the other party.

Typically the contract of sale of goods other than a retail sale across the counter begins as an " inquiry," in response to which the potential supplier gives a " tender " or " quotation." Commercially it is customary to regard such documents as not being offers, but as indications as to the terms and prices upon which an offer, made by the other party, will be likely to find acceptance by the seller. This may or may not be true in any individual case; it depends upon the wording of the documents. It will

[8] H.B. Sales, " *Standard Form Contracts* " (1953) 16 *Modern Law Review,* p. 318.

be found that where the potential purchaser is a public authority it may require the " tender " to be made in a specified form, and when this is so, the form will probably be worded so that it is legally an offer.

The purpose of this is to ensure that having received a number of competitive tenders it is in a position to convert the selected tender into a contract by the mere fact of acceptance without the tenderer having any opportunity for second thoughts, whether on price or otherwise.

In an ideally simple situation the tender will contain a quotation of the price of the goods and will specify the conditions of sale which the tenderer wishes to apply. The purchaser will accept the tender by placing his order for the goods without any qualification of the conditions and his order, which now constitutes a firm offer, will be accepted by an order acknowledgment which, again, does nothing to disturb the conditions originally set out in the tender. It is hardly necessary to say that this ideally simple situation seldom obtains in practice. Very few buying organisations can resist the temptation to print a set of " conditions of purchase " on the back of the order form, if only to say that invoices are to be rendered in triplicate and that returnable packing cases will not be paid for but returned carriage forward. It is frequently the fact that interposed between the various stages of the transactions are letters and telephone conversations which are germane to the contract. By the time the contract is regarded by the commercial or technical people concerned as having been established through an order being placed and acknowledged it is desirable for the critically minded who are concerned with the legal function to read through a number of documents and, it may be, decide how conflicting clauses can be reconciled or superimposed.

The position is hardly simplified when each party appears to have made a determined attempt from the very beginning to exclude the other's conditions. Thus an " invitation to tender " issued by a contemporary industrial organisation bears the words, printed in large type:

> Any orders placed will be covered by "purchase conditions " overleaf, and any conditions forming part of your tender that conflict shall be deemed withdrawn by your act of tendering.

Or, more emphatically still:

> Unless otherwise agreed in writing signed by a director
> or the Chief Purchasing Controller of the Purchaser, the
> Purchaser does business only on these terms and conditions
> and any Supplier who makes offers to the Purchaser or
> accepts offers made or orders placed by the Purchaser . . .
> shall be deemed to accept these terms and conditions to the
> exclusion of all others including warranties and conditions
> express or implied by law and including the Supplier's own
> terms and conditions whether or not expressly contained or
> referred to in the Supplier's offer of acceptance and notwith-
> standing any reference to the Supplier's quotation on the face
> of the Purchaser's order.

It is not unlikely that the invited tender may be made on
paper bearing the legend, "for conditions see over" and will
bear on the obverse a mass of type including a paragraph such as
the following:

> The acceptance of this tender shall be deemed to be
> acceptance of the following conditions which shall apply
> exclusively unless otherwise expressly agreed in writing.

The tender may be accepted by the issue of an order which
states that it is placed "subject to our standard conditions,"
which thus purport by reference to reintroduce the rejection of other
conditions, and the tenderer may acknowledge the order by a
similar form or words, reasserting his own conditions.

How does one find the way through this jungle? Sometimes
it seems to have become a kind of game by which each party
tries to anticipate the opponent's move and to forestall it, and
it must be admitted that the proliferation of clauses of this kind
(which are probably for the most part ineffective) tend to make
the game appear a trifle childish. Since, however, substantial
issues may hang upon the question whether a clause in a set of
conditions forms part of the contract in the event of a dispute
developing, it is necessary to seek some principle by which the
question can be decided.

On the simple question whether a clause applies, quite apart
from any purported rejection or conflict with other clauses, there
are a number of cases which have become classical because of

their considerable antiquity, although they are not completely consistent. They concern, for the most part, the conditions under which railway and steamship companies have carried passengers, the conditions being either printed on the back of the ticket or referred to thereon. As a result, they are often referred to collectively as the " ticket cases," and have made it possible to state as a generalisation that in the absence of any express agreement to the contrary, a party to a contract will be deemed to have accepted the conditions prescribed by the other party if he proceeds with the contract provided the existence of the conditions has been brought to his notice. The conventional wording of the railway ticket used to be " for conditions see over " and in the limited space on the back of the ticket all that was to be found was " issued subject to the conditions contained in the Company's timetables, waybills, and notices."

The first and principal point to be observed is that the existence of the conditions which it is desired to apply must be brought to the notice of the other party. If, as is often the case, they are printed on the obverse of the tender or order or acknowledgment, some reference should always be made on the face of the document such as " for conditions of sale see over." It does not matter, however, if they are not printed or contained within the document at all, so long as a reference to their existence is so contained and they are made available upon request. There is, however, some authority for thinking that the courts may refuse to apply provisions which are contained in conditions incorporated by reference only, or printed on a document in such a way that they are likely not to be read in detail, if those provisions are so unreasonable as to be quite beyond the contemplation of the party whose assent is to be presumed.[9] That is to say, they have ruled that the contractor who expects his contractee to take his conditions on trust is under the obligation not to include in them anything which is so foreign to the normal content of conditions in use in comparable situations as to constitute a hidden trap. In an American case [10] it was recently held that a disclaimer of responsibility by an airline was ineffective because it was printed on tickets and baggage checks in such small print as to be unreadable.

---

[9] *Parker* v. *South Eastern Railway* (1877) 2 C.P.D. 416.
[10] *Lisi* v. *Alitalia-Linee Aeree Italiane S.p.A.* U.S. Supreme Court [1968] 1 Lloyd's Rep. 505.

If in the battle of paper each rival set of conditions purports to exclude the other altogether, as in the examples quoted, it is to be presumed, although the matter has probably not been explored in the courts, that the last in the field will prevail if the other party, by his conduct, has given implied acceptance. It must, however, be offered as a *caveat* that whereas conduct can constitute an implication of acceptance, mere silence does not unless it has been expressly agreed that it shall do so. It is of no legal effect to say " unless you refuse you will be held to have accepted," except in circumstances where this course of dealing has been recognised. Thus, if the last piece of paper in the war of conditions has been an order acknowledgment purporting to accept an order under application of conditions other than those purported to be applied by the order and, if the buyer without notification to the sellers purchases his requirements elsewhere and rejects the goods when offered by the seller, the seller will not be well placed if he sues the buyer for breach of contract. The buyer may claim that the order acknowledgment was a counter offer which he did not accept and although his conduct would certainly not be in accordance with accepted commercial ethics, he might well succeed in his defence. The position would, of course, be otherwise if in the intervening period the buyer, without expressly accepting the alleged counter-offer, had shown by word or act that he recognised that a contract was in existence as, for example, by inquiring as to the date of delivery or the progress of the work.

If the rival sets of conditions are not mutually exclusive an attempt must be made to read them together. It will be found that in some respects they are complementary. The points of conflict will be identified, and in respect of those the latest to be applied will prevail.

There are, however, two very important rules of interpretation which should be kept constantly in mind in both drafting and using printed conditions, whether of sale or purchase. Each received its most classical expression in the case of *Glynn* v. *Margetson*,[11] although they have been considered and examined in many subsequent cases. It will be of interest to consider the circumstances of that case, because they are very apposite to many

[11] [1893] A.C. 351.

situations that can arise under the documents with which this book is principally concerned. It concerned a consignment of oranges shipped at a Spanish port for carriage to England. The bill of lading constituted the contract document in respect of the affreightment, and buried in the small type on the back of the bill was a clause which purported to give the owners or the master of the ship complete liberty to divert the ship and to call at any port or ports within a wide area, in any order, to take on or discharge cargo or for other reasons. Upon leaving the port at which the oranges were loaded the ship proceeded to call at other ports which were not on the normal route to England, causing considerable delay, as a result of which the oranges, being perishable, were irretrievably spoiled, involving the merchants in substantial loss. There could be no question but that the clause apparently applied to the contract, nor that the diversion and delay were within its literal wording.

The case eventually went to the Lords and the principal judgment was delivered by Lord Herschell. He drew his authority from earlier judgments going back to 1803, and as a result of his judgment supported as it was by Lord Halsbury, it can be said that these two rules apply to the interpretation of any common form contract of this kind.

     (a) Where, in the course of entering into a contract, a printed form is used upon which essential matters are written or typed into blank spaces, or letters are written by the parties which must be read in conjunction with the printed matter, the words which are written or typewritten must be given precedence over the printed matter in the event of any conflict, and, indeed, the printed clauses must in any case be read as ancillary and subservient to the written words. The essence of the thinking of the courts is that the contract consists, in the last resort, in the identity of the minds of the parties touching their intended course of action, and it is clear that words inscribed by a pen or dictated to a typist do constitute matter within the minds of the parties, whereas a printed clause on a document may not have been read by the parties for years, if at all. In the *Glynn* v. *Margetson* case the handwritten matter on the bill of lading made it clear that the consignment consisted of oranges for carriage to London. Printed clauses could therefore only be allowed to apply in so far as they could be regarded as consistent with a contract for this purpose, and as oranges were known to the shipowners to be perishable, they could not by virtue of the clause, claim a liberty to introduce delays into the voyage.

(b) The second rule is a development of this. It is that in every contract there is ultimately some basic obligation assumed by the parties, and any clause which seeks to relieve a party from the basic obligations inherent in the very existence of the contract will not be enforced by the courts. In connection with the carriage of goods, a particularly outrageous example is quoted on page 125. Such a clause, if read at its literal face value, would have the effect that the carrier accepted none of the obligations inherent in a contract for the carriage of goods. It is a clear case of the type of clause which by this rule would fail of its purpose.

These two rules should be kept well in mind by persons using and relying upon printed forms. Especially the second rule is of importance to those who set their hands to the drafting of conditions of sale and purchase. A study of actual examples makes it very clear that many draftsmen of such conditions defeat their own ends by over-reaching themselves. There is a point at which, however tightly one defends oneself behind a barricade (or is it sometimes more like a smoke screen?) of printers' ink, one has to accept responsibilities if one is to undertake business at all.

But, when all is said, it remains commonsense to make a final scrutiny of the documentation in every contract of any magnitude, and the proper time for this scrutiny is when the contract is entered into and not a year later when some argument has arisen. It is also commonsense not to rely upon printed documents with a mass of small type for provisions which are regarded as vital, but, at the cost of possible repetition, to write upon the face of the documents the provisions which are deemed to be of special importance.

4. Patents and the sale of goods

When an increasing proportion of the goods of commerce are of a technical nature, and when at any one moment there are probably 200,000 granted patents on the register, any consideration of the effect of conditions of sale or purchase upon the contract of sale would be incomplete if it failed to take notice of typical clauses relating to the possibility of the goods which are the subject of the contract infringing, or being alleged to infringe, a patent owned by a third party, and therefore exposing the buyer or the seller, or both, to an action for infringement.

If the goods are made under a patent owned by either the buyer or the seller the position is quite simple. The sale of a patented article by the owner of the patent, or by a licensee under the patent whose licence extends to the sale of the article, is considered, in the absence of any notice to the contrary by the seller, to give to the buyer by implication a licence to exercise in relation to that article all the normal rights of the owner of the patent, including the right to resell. A patented article will normally be sold to the owner of the patent only when it has been made to his express order, in which case the fact that he has ordered it to be made implies a licence to the manufacturer to manufacture it.

When, however, there is a possibility that an article may infringe a patent owned by a third party it is necessary to recognise that its sale may be an illegal act. If this is so, the contract is unenforceable and, in consequence, if the innocent buyer discovers the fact of infringement before the sale is complete, he can repudiate the contract, and if he discovers it after the sale is complete he can claim damages. The same facts can also give rise to the possibility that the seller has become liable under the provisions of the Sale of Goods Act, in particular the warranty that he has a right to sell the goods, and the conditions that the goods are of merchantable quality and, if the circumstances of the sale involve such a condition, that they are suitable for the purpose disclosed to him.

The foregoing is a simple statement of the legal position, but in practice the position is unlikely to be sufficiently simple for these principles to be applied directly. A manufacturer accused of infringement will normally allege either that the goods are not

E

within the scope of the patent, or that the patent is invalid, or perhaps both. There is therefore an inevitable uncertainty about the position, which can be resolved only by an infringement action, which is a costly and lengthy matter. This is undoubtedly why the relation between patent rights and the warranties and conditions arising under the Sale of Goods Act has not been more fully explored. The proposition that for a seller to sell goods which infringe a patent is a breach of his condition under section 12 (1) that he has a right to sell the goods, is supported only by a case which rests, not on a patent, but on a trade mark.[12] The question whether it is a breach of the implied conditions under section 14 (merchantable quality and fitness for a disclosed purpose) does not appear to have been specifically considered, but the probability appears to be that the answer would be in the negative, applying the principles laid down in a case which, though not concerned with a patent, was based upon facts in which the failure of the goods to be " merchantable," *i.e.* capable of being sold, was legal and not intrinsic.[13]

The manufacturers of technical products have found it necessary to face this matter very clearly, and in consequence have accepted and defined their responsibilities more clearly than they have done in respect of most matters arising under a contract of sale, in respect of which, as has been seen, their preoccupation has been rather to limit or exclude liabilities. Thus, in the B.E.A.M.A. conditions:

> We will indemnify you against any claim for infringement of Letters Patent, Registered Design, Trade Mark or Copyright (published at the date of the contract) by the use or sale of any article or material supplied by us to you and against all costs and damages which you may incur in any action for such infringement or for which you may become liable in any such action. Provided always that this indemnity shall not apply to any infringement which is due to our having followed a design or instruction furnished or given by you or to the use of such article or material in a manner or for a purpose or in a foreign country not specified by or disclosed to us or to any infringement which is due to the

---

[12] *Niblett* v. *Confectioners Materials Co.* [1921] 3 K.B. 387.
[13] *Sumner Permain* v. *Webb* [1972] 1 K.B. 55 (C.A.).

use of such article or material in association or combination
with any other article or material not supplied by us. And
provided also that this indemnity is conditional on your
giving to us the earliest possible notice in writing of any
claim being made or action threatened or brought against you
and on your permitting us at our own expense to conduct
any litigation that may ensue and all negotiations for a settlement of the claim. You on your part warrant that any
design or instruction furnished or given by you shall not be
such as will cause us to infringe any Letters Patent, Registered
Design, Trade Mark or Copyright in the execution of your
order.

The manufacturers have been motivated by the recognition
that it is inevitable for them to take a wide measure of responsibility for their own products in this respect, and that even if they
were not to give this explicit indemnity the discovery of any
infringement would inevitably attract the attention of the patentee
to themselves and stimulate him to initiate action. By the
inclusion of the clause they attempt to do two things. The first is
to overcome any misgivings which may exist in the mind of a
purchaser who has any cause to think that infringement is a
possibility, and the second is to ensure that in the event of any
action or threat of action the direction of strategy will from the
beginning be in their own hands. That this clause is framed on
lines that are regarded as fair to the purchaser is shown by the
fact that the corresponding clause in the I.Mech.E./I.E.E. conditions, which, as has been pointed out, represent the point of view
of a professional body favouring neither buyer nor seller, and
those of the Purchasing Officers Association follow closely the
same lines. A small, but potentially important difference, however, is the omission, in these other conditions, of the words
" published at the date of the contract." Since the publication
of a patent specification may be considerably later than the
priority date, by the parenthesis the B.E.A.M.A. conditions protect
the seller from liability to the buyer in respect of an unknown
body of patents which he may be infringing in innocence. Whilst
innocence is a permitted defence in some circumstances in a patent
action, the exclusion, in the B.E.A.M.A. conditions, of these
unpublished patents from the scope of the indemnity, makes it

possible for the buyer to be left without redress in the event of his having bought goods which, by reason of a subsequently published patent specification he can use or resell only at his peril. This, however, is not to say that the exclusion is unreasonable; it is a weakness of our patent system that this uncertainty hangs over all who, whether buyers or sellers, deal in goods of a technical nature.

It is sometimes possible for a nervous buyer to go to extremes, as for example:

> Without prejudice to other rights we may have we reserve the right to cancel this order should we receive notice alleging that any of the said goods or materials infringe against any patents trade marks or designs.

It is hardly necessary to point out that a manufacturer cannot be expected to accept a condition such as this, which would enable the buyer to cancel without notice or redress an order for articles already made to his requirements merely because of an allegation which might be quite unfounded and incapable of being justified in the courts. The clause quoted, from the B.E.A.M.A. conditions, or the corresponding clauses referred to, give assur- ances as far-reaching as any manufacturer should be expected to provide.

5. Hire-purchase contracts

For the most part, the contracts entered into in the course of retail selling lie outside the scope of this book. There is, however, one major exception to this, the hire-purchase contract, and in view of the way in which Parliament has hedged the hire-purchase transaction with safeguards for the improvident and the unwary, by laying down rules regarding the form and content of the hire- purchase contract, some comment is necessary.

In its social context " hire-purchase " is a means by which the purchaser is enabled to enjoy possession and use of the purchased article while paying for it by a series of instalments, and the term is often loosely employed to cover a number of transactions some of which are and some are not truly hire-purchase. The essence of the hire-purchase contract proper is that until the payments are complete the article is in the *possession* but not the *ownership* of the buyer, and that when the payments are complete ownership passes to the buyer either automatically or by the exercise on his part of an option to purchase it at a nominal price. In practice there is little difference between the two types of arrangement. By convention the former has sometimes been called a " hire and purchase " agreement, but by the definition of the Hire-Purchase Act 1938 either is properly called a hire-purchase agreement, the definition being,

> an agreement for the bailment of goods under which the bailor may buy the goods or under which the property in the goods will or may pass to the bailee.

It should perhaps be explained that a " bailment " exists whenever an article which is owned by one party is placed in the possession of another.

When hire-purchase as a practice began to grow it was first used as a means of obtaining business by those sellers who were strong enough financially to finance the credit which it involved, but for a considerable time now it has been the universal pattern that the hire-purchase transaction involves three parties, the seller of the goods, the buyer, and a finance company. The seller sells the goods for cash to the finance company, which hires them to the buyer under an agreement which gives the buyer the option, when the hiring period has been completed and subject to the hiring charges having been duly paid, to buy the goods for a purely nominal sum, such as £2 for a car or 50p for a refrigerator. Behind the transaction there is an agreement between the seller of the goods and the finance company, under which the seller may to some degree be entitled to act as agent for the finance company *vis-à-vis* the buyer, and may be required to undertake an obligation to indemnify the finance company in the case of certain types of default, or against the consequences of representations he may make and which by statute bind the finance company as hirer of the goods.

The agreement which is the subject of legislation as to its content and, indeed, its very format, is the agreement between the finance company and the buyer, termed for the purpose of the agreement the " owner " and the " hirer " respectively. Because this agreement is normally entered into by a printed form supplied by the finance company and prepared by its lawyers it is normal to find that it meticulously observes the requirements of the relevant statutes. These were passed in 1938, 1954 and 1964 but in the main [14] have been consolidated in the Hire-Purchase Act 1965, which now stands as the law regarding these agreements.

By statute the agreement must be prepared in such a way as to show:

(a) the cash price of the goods;

(b) the hire-purchase price of the goods, *i.e.* the total amount to be paid (including the price to be paid under the option) before property passes to the buyer;

(c) particulars of the goods sold, in sufficient detail for them to be identified;

(d) the amount of each instalment and the dates when instalments are due.

It must also contain a statement (in a form at least as prominent as the rest of the document) informing the hirer (*i.e.* the purchaser) of certain rights and obligations as set out in Schedule 1 of the 1965 Act. These are:

(a) that he may put an end to the agreement at any time by returning the goods to the owner;

(b) that he must pay instalments then due, together with such amount as will be sufficient, together with all instalments then paid, to equal half the hire-purchase price, unless the court determines that a smaller sum would be equal to the owner's loss;

(c) that if the goods have been damaged owing to the hirer having failed to take reasonable care of them, he must pay for that damage;

(d) that if the agreement contains any provisions allowing the hirer to end it on terms more favourable to him than those mentioned above he may do so;

(e) that after the hirer has paid one third of the hire-purchase price (this includes any trade-in value of goods taken in part exchange as well as deposit and instalments) the goods cannot be repossessed by the owner except with the hirer's consent or by order of the court;

(f) that in such event if the court thinks it just to do so

[14] Part III (special provisions regarding motor vehicles) and Part IV (advertisements) of the 1964 Act continue in force.

it may allow the hirer to keep some or all of the goods on such terms as it may direct.

This statement (abbreviated above) must appear in the precise form of Schedule 1, and is therefore uniform in all hire-purchase agreements. The figures constituting one half or one third of the hire-purchase price, as the case may be, are inserted as actual sums.

It has become customary for the space for the hirer's signature to be contained in a " box " with some clear indication that the document is a hire-purchase agreement, and that he signs knowing that this is so. This is to protect the vendor and the owner from the defence *non est factum* which was raised in some doorstep sales of goods to housewives who alleged that they were tricked into signing in the belief that the document was of some other nature. The Act gives protection to the hirer (purchaser) in such circumstances by providing (s. 11) that if the agreement is signed elsewhere than at " the appropriate trade premises " (which in effect means the shop or office of either the dealer or the finance company) the hirer has a statutory right to cancel it and return the goods within four days of receiving a " second statutory copy " of the agreement. This " second statutory copy " must be sent by post, and is additional to the copy of the agreement which must be handed or sent by post to the hirer whether he signs at the appropriate trade premises or anywhere else, and is in practice sent only in the case of agreements not signed at the " appropriate business premises."

As a result of these statutory requirements the hire-purchase agreement has reached a high degree of standardisation, but there is no limit to the extent to which it may be elaborated by what is so frequently designated as " small type on the back." Because the hire-purchase agreement is both technically and actually an agreement between the hirer who is the prospective purchaser on the one hand and on the other a finance company who has no interest in or control over the goods which are the subject of sale (and whose lawyers have drafted the agreement) it will be found that these small type clauses are such as to define the obligations of the hirer in relation to payments, to the custody of the goods and their insurance, while limiting or negativing so far as possible any obligations which would normally rest upon the vendor of goods or one who let goods out on hire.

The person to whom the would-be purchaser would normally look to implement the normal obligations of seller under the Sale of Goods Act or otherwise, is, of course, the dealer who has sold them. He, however, is not party to the hire-purchase agreement; nor does he sell the goods to the hirer either then or later, but to the finance company and the would-be purchaser is not privy to his agreement with that company. Thus there is no person to whom the hire-purchase customer would be able to look, under the contract, to fulfil the normal obligations of a seller. This aspect of the hire-purchase sale is dealt with in section 16 of the 1965 Act by which any person who sells goods by hire-purchase and makes any representations regarding them is deemed to be acting as the agent of the owner or seller. It is thus customary for the finance company's disavowal of obligations to be qualified by the provisions of the Act as

> " The owners do not let the goods subject to any Warranty or Condition . . . save those set out in the . . . Act."

The Act provides a protection to the prospective purchaser by imposing an implied condition that the goods are of merchantable quality, but this does not apply to goods knowingly bought as secondhand. In the typical case of the purchase of a used car by hire-purchase the maxim *caveat emptor* therefore applies almost without qualification, and the buyer has no legal protection against finding that his car is grossly defective unless he can obtain an express and written representation of its condition from the dealer himself supported by the consideration of his undertaking to buy from the finance house supporting the transaction.

In addition to the provision of the Hire-Purchase Acts as affecting the form and content of the agreements, from time to time minimum levels of deposit, expressed as proportions of the cash price, have been laid down as measures of economic policy. These lie outside the scope of this book but, of course, affect the substance of any agreement. At the time of writing none is in force.

The social purpose of the Hire-Purchase Acts was to give protection against some kinds of malpractice to the private buyer. They do not apply therefore to agreements where the hire-purchase price exceeds £2,000, nor to agreements where the hirer is a corporation. As a result of these exclusions most hire-purchase agreements made in an industrial background – and there are many – are freely negotiable between the parties. Their essential content is similar to that of the domestic hire-purchase agreement without the complications imposed on that type of agreement by law.

CHAPTER 3

CONTRACTS FOR BUILDING, ENGINEERING WORKS AND THE ERECTION OF MACHINERY

1. The standard forms

The next group of contracts which call for consideration have much in common with contracts for the sale and purchase of goods, and, indeed, shade imperceptibly into pure contracts of sale at one end of their range. Yet, fundamentally, contracts relating to building and construction are from other points of view very different from the contract of sale, and are governed by some legal assumptions and principles which do not apply to the contract for the sale of goods.

The contract for the sale of goods, however wordy it may be as a result of the zeal of the writers of " conditions of sale " or " conditions of purchase," is at root a very simple matter indeed. It is based upon the present or future existence of some thing or group of things or some ascertainable quantity of merchandise concerning which the intention of the parties is that at some moment that thing or quantity of merchandise shall cease to be the property of the seller and become the property of the buyer. The construction contract, on the other hand, presupposes no such identifiable moment. It looks to a period during which a number of physical operations will take place upon a defined piece of land – and to the lawyer land includes buildings – at the end of which period the land will include appurtenances in the shape of buildings or fixed machinery and plant which were not there before. All through the period things will be brought on to the land and some taken away therefrom. During the whole period there will be a succession of alterations of property rights.

This is due to the principle of law which is enshrined in the maxim *quicquid plantatur solo, solo cedit,* which is to say that whatever is fixed to (or planted in) the land becomes part of the land. There cannot, in English law, be a building (other than a portable building which merely rests upon the land) which belongs to a person other than the owner of the land. Where it is desired to create a situation resembling such an arrangement, as for example, where A builds on land belonging to B, the device used is a building lease, under which the land is leased at a ground rent and the leasehold interest in the erected building allowed to vest in A. But in such a situation the building is part of the land, and ultimate property rights vest in the landowner, the leaseholder's rights of ownership being derivative or temporary. The granting of a ground lease for so long a period as 999 years, a common practice in some parts of the country, renders the ultimate ownership of the building by the landowner a very shadowy concept, but the theory remains.

Another factor which tends to make the constructional contract different in form and content from the contract for the sale of goods is the frequent presence of a third party in the person of an architect, surveyor or consulting engineer. There is indeed no necessity for such an office, and many minor works are undertaken upon the basis of a contract between the owner of the land or existing buildings, on the one hand, and the building contractor, on the other, without any consultant being involved, but as the magnitude of work increases so does the probability that a consultant – architect or engineer – will be involved. This introduces a situation which can be of considerable legal interest, and one which, surprisingly, has called for examination in the courts only rarely, in that the construction contract purports to lay extensive duties upon a named person who is not a party to the contract. This point will be considered later.

Lastly, the construction contract is one in which there are frequently a number of sub-contractors. The position of the sub-contractor is capable of being a complex one, in that he is often treated by the building owner as though he were in direct contact with him, whereas the contract under which he has rights and duties is between himself and the main contractor, and the employer has no contractual relationship with him. It is obviously necessary for his rights and duties to be defined with care, and for the complicated situations brought into being by the presence on a constructional site of some dozens of sub-contractors, all to some extent reliant upon common services, to be reduced to a defined order.

For all these reasons, it is far more general for the operations involved in constructional works to be the subject of a written contract than is the case for the sale of goods. Indeed, the merchant, concerned only with buying and selling, may carry on trade for an indefinite time with little more than a perfunctory glance at the "small type on the back," but the case is very different with any contractor concerned with building or engineering construction. He is continuously negotiating contracts, and is under the necessity of reading and understanding them. This is the more necessary in that, unlike the sale of goods, building and constructional work has in general no code sanctified by statute such as the Sale of Goods Act, and in the absence of a properly detailed written contract is left to be governed only by such rules as can be invoked by custom or deduced from the common law.

As has been said, however, the two contracts can and do shade into each other. Some machinery, though completely manufactured in the factory, needs to be finally assembled and erected *in situ*. In such a case the contract is primarily one of sale and purchase, but will contain extra clauses relating to the special problems involved in erection. Extensive reference has been made in the preceding section to the conditions of sale of B.E.A.M.A., which have been used as an example of conditions competently drawn but weighted in the interest of the seller. The same association has a set of conditions for the sale of plant "inclusive of erection," which follows the same general pattern, differing substantially only in the following respects:

(a) The requirement that the purchaser will provide access to the site, foundations, scaffolding, and the necessary rough labour, lighting, and the like.

(b) A clause deals with "taking over," a concept which has to be introduced because, through the principle already explained, transfer of ownership must have taken place as the erection work proceeded, even if it had not taken place earlier.[1]

(c) Provision is made for payment to be made in instalments, with 5 per cent. being retained until one month after full completion.

[1] Such a plant is normally specially designed and custom built, and property rights probably pass under r. 5 of s. 18 of the Sale of Goods Act as soon as a manufacture of the component parts in the seller's factory is complete.

    (d) A clause limits the liability of the vendor for damages arising from accidents on site.

These provisions are superimposed, in this set of conditions, upon the basis provided by the standard conditions of the association relating to the sale of goods not involving erection. It remains avowedly a contract for the sale of goods, the price being essentially the price of the goods plus a provision for the technical labour and supervision involved in erection.

From this type of contract, however, one moves on to the type of contract which concerns the building of an installation where the work done on site is more extensive, where instead of a few large units being brought onto the site, fixed and connected up, the units brought to the site are small relative to the whole and the installation as a whole is built where it is to work. An example of such an installation would be an oil refinery or the type of plant commonly used in large-scale chemical engineering. From this the next stage may be seen in civil engineering contracts, where, although some components are brought to the site in a prefabricated state, much of the work is of a kind that could never be removed from the site without being destroyed. Lastly comes the building contract pure and simple, where without question the maxim *quicquid plantatur solo, solo cedit* undoubtedly applies and, legally, the edifice becomes for all purposes a part of the land itself.

As a result of these fundamental differences between the contract for the sale of goods and the construction contract, and the fact that there is no statutory norm such as that provided in the case of the simple sale by the Sale of Goods Act, proper documentation of the contract is more general, and the manner in which that documentation has tended to take shape is different. The paper game by which each party tries to foist its own terms on the other by sleight of hand is less evident. The inevitable complexity of the contract and the multiplicity of details which it must cover would make the task of writing such a contract, if it were to be undertaken *ab initio,* into a serious undertaking of legal draftsmanship guided by a fund of technical knowledge.

Such an undertaking is, however, seldom needed, because the very fact that the consultant, by whatever professional title called, is likely to be involved, has led to the existence of elaborate

precedents, in the shape of standard contracts. The best known
of these are:

    (a) The Model Forms of General Conditions recommended by the Institution of Mechanical Engineers, the Institution of Electrical Engineers, and the Association of Consulting Engineers for use in connection with Contracts with Erection.

    (b) The General Conditions of Contract, Forms of Tender, Agreement, and Bond, for use in connection with Works of Civil Engineering Construction, approved and recommended by the Institution of Civil Engineers, the Association of Consulting Engineers, and the Federation of Civil Engineering Contractors.

    (c) The standard Agreement and Schedule of Conditions of Building Contract, issued by the Royal Institute of British Architects.

As will be realised from what has already been said, these are
all extensive documents ranging from 15,000 to 25,000 words.
Space alone precludes their inclusion by way of reference. Each
is a serious attempt to deal with all contingencies which can be
foreseen in the class of contract with which it deals, and each is
readily available from the sponsoring association. There is a
broad similarity between them in the principles followed.

The initiative in any building contract comes from the
"employer," as the person who wishes to have the work done
is usually called. It is he who invites tenders, having engaged
his architect or consulting engineer. This official naturally and
without question invites tenders upon the basis of the standard
contracts familiar to him, and these forms have therefore become
a norm in the constructional industries. The tenderer is also
familiar with these forms, and since through his own trade
associations he has had a hand in forming them, he is unlikely to
seek to make substantial modifications. These forms therefore
have become a standard, and are far more completely recognised
and respected than is the Sale of Goods Act in the case of a
contract of sale.

Deviations from the norm established by these conditions
occur in the main when employers, especially governments,
public authorities, or very large undertakings, seek to impose
their own sets of conditions. These are generally based upon

one or other of the standards cited, but are invariably more exacting towards the contractor. In reviewing the broad lines of the standard contracts some attention will be given to the directions in which these more exacting employers try to make the provisions of the contract more stringent against the contractor.

The end products to which the three sets of conditions are directed are very different. The I.Mech.E./I.E.E. conditions are used in relation to the supply and erection of large-scale machinery installations, the I.C.E. to the building of roads, bridges, tunnels, harbour works and the like, and the R.I.B.A. to the erection of buildings. In their format they are, however, more dissimilar than they need be, because they have had a different lineage and history. The principles which each is designed to establish are in many respects identical, and it is a pity that there is not a closer accord between them as regards the language used and the order in which topics are dealt with. Almost the only respect in which they are in direct contrast is in the clause dealing with drawings,[2] the I.Mech.E./I.E.E. conditions providing that drawings will be furnished by the contractor, whereas in the I.C.E. conditions and R.I.B.A. conditions the pre-supposition is that they will be supplied by the Engineer or Architect as the case may be.

Space forbids any complete commentary upon these conditions. An admirable commentary on the R.I.B.A. conditions will be found in *Building Contracts* by Keating,[3] and a more comprehensive work on the whole subject is *Building and Civil Engineering Standard Forms* by Duncan Wallace.[4] The plan to be followed in the remainder of this chapter will be to examine in the light of these standard conditions a number of topics which stand out as of interest and also to comment on some of the ways in which, in dealing with those topics, the draftsmen of variant conditions have sought to lay more onerous duties upon the contractor. By this means it is hoped to be of practical assistance to readers whose duty it is to consider and adjudicate upon the acceptance, rejection, or modification of contract conditions offered to them.

2. Architects and engineers

The standard forms of contract which have been quoted are

---

[2] I.Mech.E./I.E.E.(A), cl. 4; I.C.E., cl. 7; R.I.B.A., cl. 3.
[3] Keating, *Law and Practice of Building Contracts*, 2nd ed., p. 257.
[4] Published by Sweet & Maxwell Ltd., 1969.

now too firmly established and too universally accepted for any fundamental changes to be expected in them. Yet it remains an anomaly that in each of them, and therefore in all the many individually drafted sets of conditions and forms of contract which are based on them, the " architect " or " engineer " appears as a person independent of both the employer and the contractor, possessing extremely wide rights and owing duties to the other parties without being himself a party to the contract in his own name. The answer which is given to explain this anomaly is that he is the agent of his client, the employer, and that the rights which vest in him do so in this capacity. This is only part of the truth, however, because it is settled law, and well recognised by the professional bodies to which architects and chartered engineers belong that in many respects they stand in the position of arbitrators between the employer and the contractor, and that they are expected to be fair and just in holding the scales between these two, who are the parties to the agreement.

The architect or engineer has a contract with the employer, and even if it has not been reduced to writing, its terms are fairly clearly implied by the very fact of his appointment in the capacity he occupies. There is, however, no privity of contract between the contractor and the architect, and although the contract between the employer and the contractor purports to lay duties upon the architect upon the performance of which the contractor relies, the contractor cannot sue the architect under the contract if he fails to perform these duties. The most obvious possibility of complaint in this regard arises if the architect unjustifiably refuses to issue a certificate for payment. The only redress available to the contractor is to sue the employer, and to be successful it is necessary for him to overcome the defence that in the absence of a certificate there is no liability under the contract for the employer to pay. In a case fought on this issue it was necessary to show that the architect had taken a wrong view of his powers, that the duty of the employer was therefore to appoint another architect, and that the employer could not take advantage of his own failure to do so.[5]

There is some safeguard, in the case of building contracts where a British architect is appointed, in the fact that architects

---

[5] *Panamena Europea Navigacion* (*Compania Limitada*) v. *Leyland* (*Frederick*) *& Co. Ltd.* (*J. Russell & Co.*) [1947] A.C. 428 (H.L.).

are, under the law of the United Kingdom, statutorily registered [6] and subject to the discipline of the Architects Registration Council. There is no such statutory registration in the case of engineers, and although in most instances the engineers appointed to supervise and control works under the I.Mech.E./I.E.E. or I.C.E. conditions are members of the various chartered bodies and therefore subject to discipline, there is nothing in the law to prevent any person from calling himself an engineer.

As one reads the various clauses of the standard conditions it becomes very evident that the powers of the architect or engineer are very extensive. He, to the exclusion of the employer himself, gives instructions to the contractor. It is his satisfaction that has to be secured, it is he who gives instructions regarding the progress of the works, he can order the dismissal of any workman of whom he disapproves, he can order variations in the works and determine adjustments as to the payment to be made therefor when the contract documents are silent, and by his power to issue certificates it is he who wields power over the payments upon which the contractor relies, and by his certification creates the financial obligations between the employer and the contractor. It is he who can decide that work is defective and must be repaired or done again, he can grant or refuse extension of time for completion, and has to act as arbitrator in many possible differences of opinion.

When one considers these extraordinary powers and realises that the person wielding them is not amenable to the contractor in any contractual relationship, it becomes evident that in his own interest the contractor should satisfy himself, first, that the architect or engineer is a person whose judgment he is prepared to trust, and secondly, that in the event of his having a serious grievance he is able to appeal to some independent authority. This is especially the case when the nominated architect or engineer is an official of an organisation or authority which is itself the employer. It is one of the fundamentals of natural justice that a man should not be a judge in his own cause, but these forms of contract come perilously near to creating precisely that situation. Even in an ordinary building contract the architect is the agent of his client, and carries a fiduciary obligation to serve his client's interest so

---

[6] By the Architects Registration Act 1938.

F

that his duty to act with fairness in a professional capacity is, as it were, superimposed upon that basic obligation. When, as in the case of a contract entered into by a local authority, which nominates its own official as architect or engineer, he is not only a professional agent but also the employee of the client, the superimposed duty calls for even more detachment, courage, and fairmindedness. It is to the credit of consultants in general that serious argument is rare.

When constructional contracts are undertaken in other countries it is important for the contractor to satisfy himself that the architect or engineer, if not a member of the United Kingdom profession, is under a similar professional code, and to find out whether, under the system of law operating in the country concerned, the same overriding obligation to exercise fairness will be judicially recognised as it is in the United Kingdom courts.[7]

In this regard the attitude taken by the courts in the United Kingdom has been established beyond question by the decision of the House of Lords in the case of *Hickman* v. *Roberts*,[8] and two passages from the individual judgments given by the Lords merit quotation. Alverstone L.J. said:

> ". . . The position of these arbitrators is a very important one . . . the system could not have been allowed to exist, had it not been found that persons in the position of engineers or architects are able to maintain, and do maintain, a fair and judicial view with regard to the rights of the parties . . . it has to be remembered that in the great majority of cases they are the agents of the employers. It has also to be remembered that they not infrequently have to adjudicate upon matters for which they themselves are partly responsible. . . . It is therefore very important that it should be understood that when a builder or contractor puts himself into the hands of an engineer or architect as arbitrator there is a very high duty on the part of that architect or that engineer to maintain his judicial position."

In the same case Shaw L.J. added:

> ". . . the position of an architect in a building contract is

---

[7] Per Fry L.J. in *Re De Morgan, Snell & Co.*, and *The Rio de Janeiro Flour Mills and Granaries Ltd.* (1892) 8 T.L.R. 292. See also *Hickman & Co.* v. *Roberts* [1913] A.C. 229 (H.L.).

[8] *Ibid.*

one of great delicacy. He is placed in that position to act judicially, when, to the knowledge of both parties, the person who is his master and his paymaster is one of the parties to the contract. It has been affirmed by courts of law, however, that that being the case his judicial position must be accepted, and it follows from that that in the peculiarly delicate situation in which such a man stands the courts of law must be particular to see that his judicial attitude is maintained."

The extent of a consultant's responsibilities has sometimes been considered by the courts. As has already been mentioned, he is not normally a party to the contract itself which stands as one governing the relations between the employer and the contractor, and it is unusual for any extensive written contract setting out his duties to be entered into between the employer and himself. It was established in a case in 1966 [9] that an architect has no power to delegate his responsibilities, and that if as a result of so doing a building proves defective, he cannot shelter behind the fact of having relied upon supposedly expert specialist designers so as to avoid personal liability.

Because of this insistence of the United Kingdom courts a general attitude has grown up in the building, contracting and engineering industries which accepts without question the authority of the consultant under a contract, in the confidence that his powers will be exercised fairly. Under other jurisdictions, however, the position both legally and by the traditions of the profession may be different, and it is therefore important in the last resort, and particularly so where the consultant is not known to the contractor, to ascertain whether a dispute with the consultant is itself referable to arbitration or to the courts. In the three sets of contract conditions under consideration as the norm the position is as follows:

I.Mech.E./I.E.E. If at any time any question dispute or difference shall arise between the Purchaser or the Engineer and the Contractor . . . the same shall be referred to the arbitration of a person to be agreed upon or failing such agreement etc. . . .

I.C.E. If any dispute . . . shall arise between the

[9] *Moresk Cleaners* v. *Hicks* [1966] 2 Lloyd's Rep. 338.

> Employer or the Engineer and the Contractor . . . it shall
> be referred to and settled by the Engineer who shall state
> his decision in writing. . . . Such decision . . . shall be
> final and binding . . . until the completion of the work. . . .
> If either the Employer or the Contractor be dissatisfied with
> any such decision of the Engineer then . . . [he] . . . may
> require that the matter be referred to an arbitrator etc. . . .
>
>   R.I.B.A. In case any dispute or difference shall arise
> between the Employer or the Architect on his behalf and the
> Contractor either during the progress or after the completion
> of or abandonment of the works as to the construction of this
> Contract or as to any matter . . . arising thereunder or in
> connection therewith (including any matter or thing left by
> this Contract to the discretion of the Architect . . .) then such
> dispute or difference shall be and is hereby referred to the
> arbitration and final decision of a person to be agreed
> between the parties etc. . . .

It will be noted that these clauses all concern the handling
of disputes with the contractor and only touch upon a disagreement between the employer and the consultant in a situation in
which this relates to some decision taken by the consultant with
which the employer differs. The least satisfactory is, perhaps,
the I.C.E. since it makes the engineer judge in his own cause with
an appeal to an independent authority only after he has carried
out his own arbitration and given his own decision, and a further
period of three months has elapsed. The R.I.B.A. is broadest
because of its inclusion within the ambit of arbitration of disputes
on matters which, by the contract, are expressly placed within
the discretion of the architect.

In each case, however, ultimate appeal is available in all
circumstances, and in most contracts placed in the United Kingdom tradition this will be found to apply. It will sometimes be
found, however, that in contracts offered in other countries the
decisions of the consultants in all matters of a technical nature
are outside the scope of the arbitration clause. Thus an elaborate
set of conditions put forward in Iraq [10] may be quoted as an
example.

---

[10] For a textile factory in Mosul in 1953.

> Whenever the Contract provision is made for any question arrangement amount matter or thing being settled decided certified or determined by the Engineer or the Engineer's Representative or resting upon or being governed or controlled by or submitted to his judgment or opinion of any of them, his or their assessment decision certificate determination judgment or opinion shall be final and conclusive for all purposes. . . .

and, in the clause providing for the settlement of disputes:

> Should the Board or the Contractor dispute any decision of the Engineer (not being a decision made final by the Contract) etc. . . . [then follow the procedural details for arbitration].

This is the kind of provision for which the contractor must be alert and which he must recognise for what it is, a naked attempt to render impossible any appeal from the absolute authority of the consultant. The same effect can be gained less obtrusively when clauses are so worded in the body of the contract as to relate to the " opinion " of the consultant with the addition, " Whose decision shall be final." With such wording all that an arbitrator can address himself to is the question " What was the opinion of the engineer?" If the contract refers to the " reasonable opinion " the question can be probed whether the opinion expressed was indeed reasonable and one is thus thrown back to the facts. Upon such subtle distinctions of wording important issues can sometimes depend.

In dealing with this kind of problem in foreign countries, especially those in which the rule of law is less evident than those of the Western tradition it is necessary to remember that the provisions of any contract are enforceable only so far as is permitted by government policy. The fact that in any jurisdiction legislation prevails over the provisions of contracts becomes specially important when the legislature is of a dictational nature.

3. Assignment and sub-letting

The general prohibition against assignment and the restriction of sub-letting which finds its place in each of the standard conditions used for illustration [11] is common to all contracts of this

[11] R.I.B.A., cl. 17; I.Mech.E./I.E.E., cl. 6; I.C.E., cl. 3.

kind, and is based upon the principle that the placing of a contract for work to be done implies some confidence in the skill of the contractor, so that it would not be a fulfilment of the contract for some other person to be allowed to do the work. There is a saving which permits the contractor to assign by way of charge or otherwise moneys becoming due to him under the contract. This is necessary because it is not unusual for a contractor to call for a bank advance in order to finance his work and to offer the payments due as security. The clause took its origin in the traditional building contract, and in its original form is perhaps a little out of touch with present-day conditions, when so much work is prefabricated and is bought by the contractor from other makers. The point at which the permissible purchase of unit items from other makers ends and the forbidden sub-letting of the contract in part begins is not easy to define. The I.Mech.E./I.E.E. conditions have attempted to tackle this aspect of the problem in this clause:

> The Contractor shall not, without the consent in writing of the Purchaser *which shall not be unreasonably withheld* assign, or transfer the Contract or the benefits or obligations thereof to any other person, provided that this shall not affect any right of the Contractor to assign either absolutely or by way of charge any moneys due or to become due to him under the Contract. The Contractor shall not without consent in writing of the Engineer *which shall not be unreasonably withheld* sub-let the Contract or any part thereof or make any sub-contract with any person or persons for the execution of any portion of the Works, *other than for materials, for minor details, or for any part of the Works of which the makers are named in the Contract.* Any such consent shall not relieve the Contractor from his obligations under the Contract.

This wording recognises the fact that no contractor can carry out a contract of the type envisaged without sub-contracting. Since he is bound to purchase from other persons components to be used in the contract, it remains uncertain how significant a " detail " can be without ceasing to be " minor." The express provision that the consent of the purchaser or the engineer is not to be unreasonably withheld is of doubtful effect without some criterion of what is reasonable. One is probably thrown back on general practice as a norm.   In practice, however, this clause gives little occasion for disagreement and causes less trouble and dispute in the drafting and agreement of forms of contract than does the allied one concerning permitted sub-contracting and the forms of sub-contract.

4. Sub-contractors and the terms of sub-contracts

The I.Mech.E./I.E.E. contract clearly envisages that the clause regarding sub-letting (providing that portions of the contract work may be sub-let by the permission of the engineer) covers the whole subject of sub-letting, because although there are references elsewhere in the conditions to sub-contractors, there is no clause corresponding with the elaborate provisions of the R.I.B.A. and I.C.E. contracts [12] regarding the position of nominated and other sub-contractors and because the definition clause defines " sub-contractor " as a person to whom any part of the contract has been sub-let with the consent of the engineer.   The R.I.B.A. and I.C.E. contracts contain clauses dealing with the position regarding nominated sub-contractors in considerable detail.

There is room for a good deal of argument in settling the terms of the sub-contractor, and in practice there is a very considerable amount of inexact and careless thinking regarding the relationship which should exist between the terms of the main contract and those of a specialist sub-contractor.   It is desirable, in order to clarify the subject, to summarise the rights and the interests of the various parties, recognising that the contract between the employer and the contractor and the contract between the contractor and the sub-contractor are distinct contracts, which legally have nothing to do with each other.

(a) The employer and his agent, the architect or engineer appointed for the contract as a whole, have the *right* to expect that the sub-contractor should assume in relation to the work he undertakes the same obligations as the main contractor, in so far as they cannot be undertaken by the main contractor himself. For example, if the main contractor is under obligation to remove from the work any workman who the

[12] R.I.B.A., cl. 27; I.C.E., cl. 49.

engineer considers to be undesirable [13] or incompetent, the main contractor will be expected to bind his sub-contractor in like sense.

(b)   It is in the *interest* of the main contractor to pass on to the sub-contractor as many of the burdens placed upon him by the employer as he can, but he has no *right* to do so.   One of his functions as main contractor, in consideration of which he is expected and entitled to take a profit upon the cost of sub-contracts, is to bear the impact of any differences between the terms of the contract which he has negotiated with the employer and that which he is able to negotiate with the sub-contractor.   The contractor has a *right*, however, not to be forced into an unreasonably harsh (to him) contract with a sub-contractor merely because the employer has nominated the sub-contractor and the sub-contractor has proved to be intransigent in negotiation.

(c)   The sub-contractor has the *right* subject to the foregoing to negotiate his own contract in terms that are properly applicable to his own industry and its products.

(d)   In matters of payment the main contract and the sub-contract are independent.   The sub-contractor looks to the main contractor for payment, and unless specially agreed, has no interest in the payments made by the employer to the main contractor.

There is a tendency for main contractors to endeavour to pass on all the terms of the main contract (which is natural) and to do so by short-cut methods which appear to make critical examination of the contract unnecessary (which is lazy).   Sometimes, for example, it is considered sufficient for a sub-contractor to be invited to quote upon the general indication that the terms of the main contract will apply to all sub-contracts, and sometimes he is not even furnished with a copy of the contract terms, being expected either to take them on trust, or, if he so wishes, to examine them at the main contractor's office.

A more formal and precise method is that provided by the

[13] I.C.E., cl. 16.

form of specimen contract published by the National Federation of Building Trades Employers and the Federation of Associations of Specialists and Sub-Contractors. This is primarily designed to be used where the main contract is in the R.I.B.A. form, and has the advantage of certainty over the vague expressions sometimes used in the manner suggested above. Whilst it has its place in the building and contracting industry, it has certain disadvantages from the point of view of the sub-contractor.

    (a) It merely recites that the " Sub-contractor has had reasonable opportunity of inspecting the Main Contract or a copy thereof," and upon this basis requires him to " be deemed to have notice of all the provisions of the Main Contract . . ." [14] and requires him to " observe, confirm and comply with all the provisions of the Main Contract . . . so far as they relate and apply to the Sub-contract works and are not repugnant to or inconsistent with the express provisions of this Sub-contract as if all the same were severally set out herein." [15] No express right is given to the Sub-contractor to inspect the terms of the Main Contract at all reasonable times. It is submitted that if the Sub-contractor is to observe provisions which are imposed by reference to the Main Contract he ought to be given a copy of these provisions.

    (b) It still leaves the parties to decide which provisions do in fact relate to the Sub-contract, and in this respect is in the last resort little more precise than the vague expressions already criticised.

    (c) In some circumstances the variations clause could be unreasonably exacting. The main contractor is himself protected by the close definition of " variations " in the R.I.B.A. contract (where this is the form of the main contract) and, in the case of the I.C.E. and I.Mech.E./I.E.E. contract, by the introduction of a limiting percentage to the permissible variations. This protection is not passed on and there is no limit

[14] s. 1.
[15] s. 3.

either in kind or quantity to the variations which are to be effected " forthwith." [16]

(d) The Sub-contractor, having signed the contract, has to await the issue of an " order " from the contractor, upon the receipt of which he is required to commence the work " within seven days." [17] This would be quite impracticable in many industries when factory production must be planned well ahead and where the skilled labour required for installation work cannot be held in reserve and must be moved from job to job in accordance with a pre-arranged time-table.

(e) Time is made of the essence of the contract by the provision that " if the Sub-contractor fails to complete the Sub-contract works within the period specified ... he shall pay to the Contractor any loss or damage suffered or incurred by the Contractor and caused by the failure of the Contractor as aforesaid of which loss or damage the Contractor shall at the earliest opportunity give reasonable notice. ...." This could bear with undue rigour upon a Sub-contractor and will be discussed later under " Liquidated Damages."

The tendency to require sub-contractors to assume all the obligations of the main contract, whether in vague and general terms or through the medium of this form of sub-contract has been strongly opposed in some quarters. A trade bulletin circulating in the electrical industry [18] has contained the following strictures:

The . . . Committee frequently has to consider the case when a main contractor attempts to impose on a sub-contractor a set of unsuitable conditions on the grounds that these are the conditions which the main contractor has to accept. Sometimes this is done by a short form of words in which the sub-contractor is asked to accept the terms of the main contract in so far as they apply to him. On other

---

[16] s. 7: " In the event of the Contractor (a) requiring . . . any variations in the Sub-contract works; or (b) issuing . . . any instructions of the Architect in relation to the Sub-contract, then the Sub-contractor shall forthwith comply with and carry out the same in all respects accordingly."

[17] s. 8.

[18] British Electrical and Allied Manufacturers Association.

occasions attempts are made to construct a garbled set of sub-contract conditions based on the main contract.

Both these methods are equally unsatisfactory and in the event of a dispute can lead to difficult problems of interpretation and construction. . . . The worst types of case arise when attempts are made to place orders for the supply of engineering goods as part of an overall civil engineering contract. There are, however, many other less extreme instances of this form of abuse occurring every day. A common one is to attempt to apply a set of erection conditions governing the main contract to sub-contractors who are delivering equipment only and have no erection to do.

In some fields an attempt has been made to overcome the sub-contracting problems by introducing a single special set of standard sub-contract conditions for use with standard main contracts. This has never been a method which can be applied in the engineering industries. The variety of sub-contracts is infinite and it is impossible to provide one standard form which would do for all.

It cannot be too frequently repeated that " this is in the main contract so we must pass it on to you " is not a valid reason. The main contractor takes special risks and in his negotiation with his purchaser he should see to it that a contingency is built in to deal with these risks. One such is the potential liability arising from differences between the conditions of contract he accepts and the conditions under which he makes his purchases. The latter may well be dictated by long-standing practice. It is no substitute to omit an appropriate contingency and then attempt to make up for bad estimating by equally bad sub-contract practice.

The recommendation offered by this bulletin is that the standard conditions accepted as suited to the work being done (as, for example, the I.Mech.E./I.E.E. in the case of mechanical or electrical engineering works) should be used, any special obligations arising from the special circumstances or the provisions which the main contractor has underwritten in the main contract being included by way of an addendum. There is good sense in this recommendation, and the attempt to safeguard the main contractor by the omnibus provision that the terms of the main contract apply can lead to confusion in interpretation.

In one respect, however, as has been pointed out, the main contractor has the right not to be held to ransom by an intransigent sub-contractor who considers himself in a strong position by reason of having been nominated by the employer. This is given by the R.I.B.A. contract in the clause [19] which provides that " the Architect shall not nominate any person as a sub-contractor . . . who will not enter into a sub-contract which provides (*inter alia*) . . ." and then follow a number of sub-clauses which ensure that the principal obligations of the main contractor will be underwritten by the sub-contractor in so far as they relate to the work undertaken by the sub-contractor. The actual contract between contractor and sub-contractor is, however, properly left to be negotiated between them, and there is provision for the waiving of any of the listed requirements by agreement between the main contractor and architect. The net result is that the sub-contract is to be regarded as being negotiated individually between the contractor and sub-contractor, but if the latter refuses to accept obligations meeting the listed requirements the contractor is not under compulsion in the matter. Such a provision is fair and reasonable.

5. Variations

In the contract for the sale of goods it is of the essence of the contract that the goods which are the subject of the contract should be ascertainable, if not indeed at the time the contract is made, by the time the contract is carried out and in accordance with criteria established at the time the contract is entered into. The contract for building, civil engineering or erection of machinery, on the other hand, is entered into in the clear recognition that the building or installation which is to be brought into being exists only in the mind of the designer and that during the time which will elapse between the signing of the contract and its completion, changes in the design may be decided upon or may be forced upon the architect or engineer by circumstances. They may arise from a variety of causes. The architect or engineer may have second thoughts, difficulties may be met which necessitate

[19] R.I.B.A., cl. 27.

a change of design, or the plans prepared at the time when the contract is signed may not have been fully worked out in detail. Very often, for example, it is not practicable to decide upon cable layouts for electrical services until major works have progressed. This fact is the reason for the clause which appears in all such contracts regarding variations. Its interpretation can give rise to some subtle and interesting questions which, however, do not seem to have been fully explored in the courts.

The three common form contracts, which are being treated as constituting the standard from which deviations may be made in practice, themselves differ in some degree in the treatment of variations. In the R.I.B.A.[20] " Variations " is defined as meaning the " alteration or modification of the design quality or quantity of the Works as shown in the Contract Drawings and described by or referred to in the Contract Bills " (*i.e.* Bills of Quantities) and includes " *the addition, omission or substitution of any work* . . ." (" work " in the R.I.B.A. conditions is not a defined term). This definition, coupled with the provision that " the Architect may issue instructions requiring a variation . . ." has the effect that there is no definable limit to the kind or the quantity of work which the contractor may be called upon to undertake, unless it is quite clearly outside the general description of " the Works " in the contract itself. Thus it would not be a permissible " variation " of a contract for building houses to require the contractor to build a factory instead, but so long as what was being built remained within the general description contained in the form of contract almost any deviation in respect of design, materials, or method of construction would be within the clause.

In the I.C.E. contract [21] the nature of the permitted variations is much more clearly defined. In the first place the variations must be variations in the form, quality, or quantity of the " Works " and " the Works" are defined as being " the Works to be executed in accordance with the Contract " and the " Contract " as the " General Conditions, Specifications, Drawings, priced Bill of Quantities, Schedule of Rates and Prices (if any) and the Contract Agreement." Further, the contract lays down five categories of variations;

[20] Cl. 11.
[21] Cl. 51.

(a) increase or decrease the quantity of any work included in the contract,
(b) omit any such work,
(c) change the character or quality of any such work,
(d) change the levels, lines, positions, and dimensions of any part of the works, and
(e) execute additional work of any kind necessary for the completion of the " Works."

These are widely and inclusively drawn, but remain firmly linked to the " Works " as defined.

The I.Mech.E./I.E.E. contract is much narrower in its scope. Like the I.C.E. contract, it gives the engineer power to " direct the contractors to alter, amend, omit, add to or otherwise vary any of the Works " and the " Works " are defined as " all plant to be provided and work to be done by the Contractor under the Contract." The variations clause,[22] however, continues with the proviso " that no variations shall, except with the consent in writing of the contractor, be such as will *with any variations already directed to be made involve* a net increase or decrease in the Contract Price of more than 10 per cent. thereof."

This limiting percentage is a valuable protection to the contractor, since without it he may be required to continue work of any particular type indefinitely, at the price included in his quotation notwithstanding that the price might be uneconomic, either by miscalculation or by changes in costs since the contract was quoted for. The words italicised above are important, and are sometimes omitted, to the disadvantage of the contractor. Thus, one set of conditions [23] based broadly on the same model is qualified by the words:

> Provided that no alteration, amendment, omission, addition or variation shall, except with the consent in writing of the Contractor, be such as will involve an increase or decrease of the total price payable under the Contract by more than 10 per cent. thereof.

It is submitted that whatever may be the intention of such a clause its effect if strictly construed would be to permit an

---

[22] Cl. 10.
[23] The Electricity Commission of New South Wales.

unlimited number of variations provided that no one variation exceeded 10 per cent. of the contract in value.

There is some authority [24] for saying that in a contract to do a specified work for a lump sum the omission of anything necessary for the completion of the work from the specification put forward by the contractor as the basis of his offer will not enable the omitted work to be charged for as an extra. This is why a set of conditions drafted quite frankly in the interest of the contractor [25] includes the clause " Limits of Contract – Our tender includes only such goods, accessories and works as are specified therein."

In practice, the question whether works called for as variations are properly so regarded is seldom considered except when there is a limiting percentage (as in the I.Mech.E. / I.E.E. conditions) and the opportunity is taken by the contractor to negotiate a new price when costs have increased in the intervening period. It can in some circumstances become important, however, because a true variation within the terms of the contract can be required as of right and will be paid for at schedule rates or at a price fixed by the architect or engineer. If a variation is not within the scope of the contract the contractor can refuse to undertake it or can negotiate his price as though it were a separate contract (as, indeed, it is). This circumstance can arise when a limiting percentage has been reached. It can also arise, although the fact that it has arisen cannot be so precisely demonstrated, when the variations have so greatly exceeded anything that could have been anticipated as to reach a magnitude which was clearly not within the contemplation of the parties when the contract was entered into.[26] It can also, and more significantly, arise when the variations involve work of a different kind from that included in the contract. " Either the additional work or varied work . . . is the kind of additional or varied work contemplated by the contract or it is not. . . . If it was . . . so peculiar, so unexpected, and so different from what any person reckoned or calculated upon that it is not within the contract at all . . . or [the contractor] might have said ' I entirely refuse to go on with the contract . . .

24 *Williams* v. *Fitzmaurice* (1858) 3 H. & N. 844.
25 B.E.A.M.A. " B," Conditions of sale for goods for use in the United Kingdom inclusive of Erection.
26 *Parkinson (Sir Lindsay) & Co.* v. *H.M. Commissioner of Works and Public Buildings* [1949] 2 K.B. 632.

or if I do it must be paid a *quantum meruit.*' " [27]   When, however,
work has been done on a variation order without objection by the
contractor there is probably an estoppel that would prevent his
arguing later that it was not within the scope of the variation
clause.

6. Vesting of plant

Construction contracts frequently contain a clause or clauses
(sometimes, as in the case of the I.C.E., worked out with great
precision) [28] which purport to have the effect of causing materials
and plant to become the property of the employer when brought
on to the site, and to preclude their being taken off the site without
the consent of the architect or engineer, and which provide that
they shall re-vest in the contractor when, with the consent of the
architect or engineer, they are removed from the site.   One
purpose of such clauses is to protect the employer from danger of
excessive dislocation to his work in the event of the contractor
becoming insolvent, since by virtue of the materials and plant
being the property of the employer they would in such case be
available for use by a new contractor and without the provision
might be seized by creditors.   In practice, the clauses in question [29]
are accepted without much consideration of their ultimate legal
validity or their precise effect, and since contractors do not undertake contracts in the expectation of becoming insolvent, they are
seldom invoked.   In so far as they relate to materials and plant
brought onto the site with the intention of being incorporated into
the works which are the subject of the contract they are reasonable, especially as, in any event, by incorporation into the construction they would ultimately become the property of the
employer.   The position is different in the case of tackle, tools,
and constructional plant, and whilst the protection to the employer
given in the event of the insolvency of the contractor is the main
consideration, the rights of the contractor in the event of the insolvency of the employer are not dealt with in the forms of contract.
In practice, the right of the contractor to have tackle, tools, or
constructional plant re-vested in him would be safeguarded in the
event of the insolvency of the purchaser, by the architect or

[27] *Thorn* v. *Mayor and Commonalty of London* (1876) 1 App.Cas. 120.
[28] I.C.E., cl. 53.
[29] I.C.E., cl. 53; I.Mech.E./I.E.E., cl. 17.

engineer giving permission for it to be removed from the site, in which event re-vesting would flow as an automatic consequence, or by the fact that the liquidator or trustee in bankruptcy would only possess the goods subject to the contractual obligation to re-vest them in the contractor at the completion of the work or at the termination of the contract.   It has also been argued that the presence of clauses inconsistent with the ownership of the con-structional plant and tools by the purchaser throws doubt on the validity of the vesting clauses.   The most elaborate of the clauses under consideration is that contained in the I.C.E. conditions,[30] which specially deals with plant hired by the contractor or on hire-purchase, providing that this will, in the event of the insol-vency of the contractor, be placed at the disposal of the employer. The I.C.E. clause, however, uses the phrase " *be deemed to become* the property of the Employer," and there is some doubt whether it is in fact effective to transfer rights of property.[31] Variants of these clauses normally follow the same general lines, and need no comment.

7. Liability for loss or damage and insurance

These two subjects are closely linked together, and therefore there is some advantage in dealing with them together.

All construction contracts lay upon the contractor certain liabilities in respect of damage to property and personal injuries arising out of execution of the works, and the fact that this is so suggests that the intention is to require him to bear a greater degree of responsibility than would be the case in the absence of express provisions.   It is therefore desirable to have clearly in mind the extent of his liability under common law in the absence of express provisions in the contract document.   In brief, the position under common law is that he would be responsible for:

>   (a) any injury or damage to third parties arising from the carrying on of the work, as for example, if he were to trespass upon land to which he was not entitled to have access, if the works caused damage by under-mining or removing support from neighbouring

[30] I.C.E., cl. 53.
[31] *Bennett and White (Calgary)* v. *Municipal District of Sugar City No. 5* [1951] A.C. 786 (P.C.).

property, or if the noise created by the work were such as to be a nuisance;

(b) any injury or damage to any persons, whether a third party, or the employer or architect or their employees or agents, or to fellow contractors arising from his negligence.

It will now be of interest to compare the effect of the following two clauses, the former taken from the I.Mech.E./I.E.E. and the latter from the R.I.B.A. conditions.

(*a*) The Contractor shall, subject to sub-clauses (vi) and (vii) of this clause indemnify the Purchaser in respect of all damage or injury occurring before all the Works shall have been taken over under clause 27 to any person or any property (other than property forming part of the Works) and against all actions, suits, claims, demands, costs, charges, and expenses arising in connection therewith *which shall be occasioned by the negligence of the Contractor* or any Sub-contractor, or by defective design (other than a design made, furnished or specified by the Purchaser and for which the Contractor has disclaimed responsibility in writing within a reasonable time after the receipt of the Purchaser's instructions) materials or workmanship, but not otherwise.[32]

(*b*) The Contractor shall be liable for, and shall indemnify the Employer against any liability, loss, claim or proceedings whatsoever arising under any statute or at common law in respect of personal injury or for the death of any person whomsoever *arising out of or in the course of or caused by the carrying out of the Works, unless due to any act or neglect of the Employer* or of any person for whom the Employer is responsible.[33]

The words italicised indicate the essential contrast between the two clauses, and illustrate a very important point which should receive attention in the scrutiny of contract terms. In the first example the liability to indemnify arises only in the event of the contractor's negligence, whereas in the latter there is no need for any party to be negligent, or indeed for the cause of an accident to be traced, to bring the indemnity into effect. It is possible to envisage circumstances where negligence cannot be proved, or

[32] I.Mech.E./I.E.E., cl. 21 (iv).   [33] R.I.B.A., cl. 18 (I).

where although it is clear that there has been negligence it cannot be fastened upon the contractor. When special conditions are written in the interest of the employer the clause is liable to become much more exacting. Thus, in framing conditions otherwise based upon the I.Mech.E./I.E.E. one large purchaser[34] substitutes for the clause quoted above:

> The Contractor shall take every practicable precaution not to damage or injure any adjoining or other property or any persons and in the event of any such damage or injury arising out of or in consequence of the execution or maintenance of the Works the Contractor shall satisfy all claims made arising therefrom whether made by the Employer or by a third party against the Contractor and/or Employer and the Contractor shall indemnify the Employer from and against all actions, suits, claims, demands, damages, costs, charges and expenses arising in connection therewith. Providing always that nothing herein contained shall be deemed to render the Contractor liable for or in respect of or to indemnify the Employer against any compensation or damages for or with respect to injuries or damage to persons or property resulting from any act or neglect of the Employer, his agents, servants or other contractors (not being employed by the Contractor).

It will be noted that in the I.Mech.E./I.E.E. clause no liability arises unless there is negligence on the part of the contractor, so that if an action brought against the employer fails to establish that there was negligence on the part of the contractor the indemnity will not arise and the employer will be left to bear his own costs in so far as they are not recoverable from the claimant. Under the quoted variant, on the other hand, the contractor has to " satisfy all claims made against either himself or the employer arising in connection with the Works," which could be an onerous burden.

It is sufficiently burdensome for the contractor to be obliged to deal with, and indemnify the employer against, claims based upon alleged but unproved negligence, but it is possible for heavily weighted conditions to go further. Thus:

[34] *Imperial Chemical Industries Ltd., General Conditions of Contract for Electrical and Mechanical Engineering Contracts*, ed. 1961, cl. 21 (iii).

> Should the Board have to pay or *elect to pay* any money in respect of any such claim or demands as aforesaid the amount so paid and the costs incurred by the Board shall be charged to and paid by the Contractor and the Contractor shall not be at liberty to dispute or question the right of the Board to make such payment notwithstanding the same may have been made without its consent or authority, and notwithstanding any decision or determination in law or otherwise to the contrary.[35]

This type of clause, it is hardly necessary to say, should be rejected by the contractor, since he would have no redress against the employer entertaining the most frivolous claims and making unlimited payments at his expense. It is surprising, indeed to find that conditions of this kind can be issued bearing the names of consulting engineers of international standing.

Apart from the kind of damage or injury referred to in the foregoing paragraphs, the contractor may be held liable to make good damage occurring to the work itself from a variety of causes, which vary as between various types of contract. Of the common form contracts which in this section are taken as the norm the most exacting upon the contractor is the I.C.E., which provides:

> From the commencement to the completion of the Works the Contractor shall take full responsibility for the care thereof and of all Temporary Works and in case any damage loss or injury shall happen to the Works or to any part thereof or to any Temporary Works from any cause whatsoever (save and except the excepted risks as defined in sub-clause (2) of this clause) shall at his own cost repair and make good the same so that at completion the Works shall be in good order and condition and in conformity in every respect with the requirements of the Contract and the Engineer's instructions. In the event of any such damage loss or injury happening from any of the excepted risks the Contractor shall if and to the extent required by the Engineer and subject always to the provisions of clause 65 hereof repair and make good the same as aforesaid at the cost of the Employer. The Contractor shall also be liable for any damage to the Works

---

[35] Quoted from conditions put forward by the Government of Iraq Development Board.

occasioned by him in the course of any operations carried out by him for the purpose of complying with his obligations under clause 49 thereof.

(2) The " excepted risks " are riot (in so far as it is uninsurable) war invasion act of foreign enemies hostilities (whether war be declared or not) civil war rebellion revolution insurrection or military or usurped power or a cause solely due to use or occupation by the Employer of any portion of the Works in respect of which a Certificate of Completion had been issued or a cause solely due to the Engineer's design of the Works (all of which are herein collectively referred to as the " excepted risks ").[36]

The " excepted risks," it will be observed, are in this case those against which it is not possible to insure, so that it can be assumed with fair confidence that provided the proper facilities are used to obtain insurance cover, the contractor is not exposed to any undue or unreasonable risk.[37] That risk can arise, however, if the liabilities clause is so wide as to include obligations that cannot be insured against.   Thus in one set of conditions [38]:

The contractor shall be responsible for all loss damage or depreciation to the plant until the plant is taken over in accordance with clause 32.

This is all-inclusive. The conditions require the contractor to insure with the Government Insurance Fund of the state for which the works are being carried out against " all insurance risks for loss or damage in transit and for all extraordinary risks like destruction or damage by fire, flood, storm, riot or civil commotion." It is not difficult to conceive of classes of damage not falling within the insurance requirement, some indeed not in any event insurable, which could involve loss to the contractor through the operation of the all-inclusive liabilities clause. Especially is this the case if the word " depreciation " in that clause is given due weight. A clause of this kind introduces a temptation for the employing authority to use every artifice to delay take-over, so that

[36] I.C.E., cl. 20.
[37] The possibility of works being seriously damaged by earth movements or subsidence during the period for which the contractor is responsible, such subsidence not being due to any default on the part of the contractor, is sometimes overlooked.
[38] Bombay Electricity Board.

the cost of depreciation during a prolonged period may be shifted to the contractor's shoulders.

The obligation to insure is invariably laid upon the contractor, and it is noticeable that this obligation is one into which the many forms of contract conditions, prepared for individual buyers but based broadly upon the "common form" contracts, introduce individual variations. It is a wise precaution on the part of the contractor in any case where doubt is felt to submit the appropriate clauses in full to his insurers for their approval. Frequently the conditions are written upon the assumption that a separate policy will be written for the contract and it is required that the interest of the employer shall be noted in the policy and the policy produced for his inspection. This can be a nuisance in the case of a contracting organisation which, as is usual, carries omnibus policies covering all its works in a single underwriting, and especially so in the case of specialist sub-contractors who at any one time are concerned with a large number of relatively small contracts, rather than with a small number of large contracts as tends to be the case with the main contractors. Although in most cases a certificate from the insurers, or from insurance brokers, or even from the contractor himself is acceptable in lieu of the indorsement of a special policy, the employer does sometimes stand upon his rights in the matter, and especially so where the employing authority is a government with an interest in its own national insurance undertaking.

It is important to remember that the contractor's normal fire policy may cover the work upon which he is engaged, but will not protect him against any liability he may have if fire commencing within his own section of the works spreads to the property of others. If the fire is attributable to negligence on his part or on the part of his servants or agents he may be involved by subrogation in a claim from the fire insurers who have insured the damaged property. For this reason it is important for the contractor to give attention to the maximum indemnity provided by his third party policy. It has become customary for this maximum to be very high, often running into millions of pounds, and any lower figure, whilst saving marginally on premiums, can expose the contractor to a risk which, although remote, could be quite disastrous.

The counsel of prudence in respect of the whole matter of

liability for injury or damage and the obligation to insure, is to read the contract carefully, and in the event of any misgivings to allow one's insurers to examine it and seek an undertaking that all the insurable risks involved are underwritten. If any risks cannot be insured they should not be accepted at all.

8. Extension of time for completion

As has been seen, in the simple contract for the sale of goods the statute has implied, and the decisions of the courts have tended to confirm, that, in the absence of any indication to the contrary, times quoted as part of the contract, other than those relating to payments, are of the essence of the contract.[39] Unlike the contract for the sale of goods, the law relating to building contracts has never been codified, but it is clear that upon general principles any time quoted for the completion of the work, or for the attainment of any specific stage in the process of completion is " of the essence of the contract " in the sense that failure to comply with the undertakings given in relation to completion entitle the aggrieved party to claim that the defaulter is in breach of the contract, and to sue him for damages, and, taking an extreme view, which in practice would only be taken in the case of a most serious default, entitle him to eject the contractor from the contract so that the work can be completed by another. In such an event the vesting clause, which has already been commented upon, may operate so as to enable the employer to require all plant, tools and tackle and all unfixed material to be left upon the site for the new contractor to use.

Each of the three common form contracts which are here taken as standard provide for the declaration of a time for completion. In the R.I.B.A. contract it is included as a schedule, and incorporated by reference.[40] In the I.Mech.E./I.E.E. conditions there is no such provision, but reference is made to the "time fixed by the Contract " and by definition the " Contract " includes " all documents to which reference may properly be made, in order to ascertain the rights and the obligations of the parties." This may leave the obligation of the contractor for the completion to be spelled out from correspondence, although in many cases

[39] Sale of Goods Act 1893, s. 10 (1).
[40] R.I.B.A., cl. 21 (1).

there will have been a tender form which calls for a specific and precise undertaking. The I.C.E. form provides a " form of tender," [41] one line of which calls for a declaration of the time for completion, and requires that the work be completed within that time.

It will sometimes be found that the contract terms are made more explicit as regards the obligation to complete by the time quoted. Thus the General Conditions of Government Contracts for Building and Civil Engineering Works, published by H.M. Stationery Office, provide that, " The works shall be carried on and completed to the satisfaction of the Supervising Officer and delivered up in a perfect state to his satisfaction on or before the date for completion." The clause dealing with " Damages for Delay " commences with the words, " Time being of the essence of the contract . . . ," and a further clause expressly provides that the authority (*i.e.* the employing department) can determine the contract:

> . . . if the Contractor shall delay or suspend the execution of the Works so that either in the judgment of the Supervising Officer he will be unable to secure the completion of the Works by the date for Completion or he has already failed to complete the Works by that date.

In an Indian contract:

> The time allowed for carrying out the work as entered in the tender shall be strictly observed by the contractor. The work shall throughout the stipulated period of the contract proceed with (*sic*) all diligence time being deemed to be of the essence of the contract on the part of the contractor. . . .[42]

The addition of this type of clause, however, only makes additionally clear what is already the position if a time has been quoted, and it should be noted that if the R.I.B.A. or I.C.E. forms are used, and a time quoted in a tender letter is inserted in the schedule or tender form attached to the contract, the contractor may find it difficult at a later date to rely upon qualifications or escape clauses which he may have included in

[41] I.C.E., cl. 43.
[42] Bombay Electricity Board.

correspondence. The completion of a document of such a kind as provided by these forms is regarded as superseding and summing up all previous correspondence and negotiations, and it may be difficult, in the case of a subsequent argument, to persuade the court or the architect to look beyond it.

Looking at the matter from the point of view of the employers, the observance of quoted times is seen to be vitally important. The date for completion is often more important than the price quoted in reaching a decision for placing a contract which has been open to competitive tender. The completion or non-completion of civil works involved in a drainage or irrigation scheme before the time for a sowing or harvest can involve a government in gains or losses far outweighing any difference between the quoted prices. Similarly, the non-completion of a contract for erection of productive machinery can involve a buyer in losses of production much greater than could be compensated by the monetary advantage of a cheaper price. Unless therefore the buyer adopts a strict attitude in the matter of compliance with quoted times there is a danger of early completion dates being quoted irresponsibly in order to obtain contracts. Even where there is a " penalty " clause, there is a temptation for the irresponsible contractor, who knows that the contract will be awarded on the basis of completion times rather than on price, to quote an impracticable early completion date, inflating his price to cover the damages which he realises he may have to pay.

A time for completion is therefore quoted. By actual inclusion in the contract or by reference it forms part of the contract. It is clear, however, that at the moment of signing a contract for building or engineering works, the whole picture of the operation is far from clear, and there are many foreseeable contingencies which may affect the course of events. Every contract must therefore make provision for an adjustment of the date in the event of these contingencies rendering completion impossible within the time. Examples of the causes which may be invoked as entitling the contractor to an extension are:

    (a) *Arising from the act or default of the employer*
        Delay in giving access to the site.
        Variations or additions to the work.
        Delay in giving particulars or decisions.

(b) *Arising from natural causes*
    Inclement weather (as affecting outdoor work).
    Flood.
    Earthquake.
(c) *Arising from accident*
    Fire.
(d) *Arising from circumstances extraneous to the parties*
    Industrial dispute.
    Riot or civil commotion.

This list is by no means exhaustive, and it will be found that typical contracts vary in the contingencies which they include in the list. Not only are there differences between the common form contracts, but many other variations will be found in contracts individually drawn.

In scrutinising contracts from the point of view of the contractor, the important consideration is to be sure that the clauses are sufficiently widely drawn to include all contingencies that can be foreseen as being likely to give proper and reasonable justifications for failure to complete on time, and this is best secured not with a multitude of words, but with an inclusive phrase such as " circumstances beyond the reasonable control of the contractor." A phrase frequently found, especially in foreign contracts, but also with increasing frequency in contracts in the United Kingdom is *force majeure*. The precise meaning of this phrase was considered in *Lebeaupin* v. *Crispin*.[43] Its meaning in French law was stated to be " all circumstances independent of the will of man, and which it is not in his power to control. . . ." Thus war, inundations, and epidemics are cases of *force majeure*: it has even been decided that a strike of workmen constitutes a case of *force majeure*. The case showed, however, that the phrase has no clearly defined meaning in English law and must be interpreted in each contract by reference to its context. In the R.I.B.A. contract it appears as one of a list of causes of delay, the others being exceptionally inclement weather, fire, civil commotion, trade disputes, and a number of other causes falling within the first group mentioned previously as arising from the act or default of the employer. Since its proper meaning as derived from French law would include many of the other causes

---

[43] [1920] 2 K.B. 714. See also *Matsoukis* v. *Priestman & Co.* [1915] 1 K.B. 681.

specifically mentioned, one is left the option of giving the phrase its proper meaning and thus regarding the mention of the others as tautological or giving it a much narrower meaning comparable with that of *vis major* which properly refers to the interference of persons possessing superior power either legally or by the use of violence. It may therefore be concluded that the use of the phrase *force majeure* gives a wider protection to the contractor if it stands alone than if there were added to it, as is often done, half a dozen assorted difficulties which occur to the draftsman's mind. If it is felt desirable to mention these specific hazards as well as *force majeure*, they should be mentioned as being *included within* the meaning of *force majeure* and not as additional to it. Further, some such phrase as *inter alia* should be introduced to show that the named hazards do not constitute an exhaustive definition, thus ". . . *force majeure* which expression shall be deemed to include *inter alia* flood storms earthquake riot etc. . . ." Even so, it is best to leave it on its own, because to mention these other specific hazards may set up the *ejusdem generis* rule of interpretation so that anything not mentioned specifically but to be included must be *of the same kind* as the things mentioned. As an illustration of this principle of interpretation " flutes, violins and other instruments " would include clarinets but not voltmeters, " voltmeters, ammeters and other instruments " would include power-factor indicators but not violins.

It is interesting to compare the three sets of conditions in respect of the granting of extensions of time:

> R.I.B.A., clause 23. Upon it becoming reasonably apparent that the progress of the Works is delayed, the Contractor shall forthwith give written notice of the cause of delay to the Architect, and if in the opinion of the Architect the completion of the Works is likely to be or has been delayed beyond the Date for Completion stated in the appendix to these Conditions or beyond any extended time previously fixed under either this clause or clause 33 (1) (c) of these Conditions,[44]
>
> (a) by *force majeure*, or
> (b) by reason of any exceptionally inclement weather, or
> (c) by reason of loss or damage occasioned by one or

---

[44] Which relates to war damage.

more of the contingencies referred to in clause 20 [A] [B] or [C] of these Conditions (*i.e.* fire, flood etc.), or

(d) by reason of civil commotion, local combination of workmen, strike or lockout affecting any of the trades employed upon the Works or any of the trades engaged in the preparation, manufacture or transportation of any of the goods or materials required for the Works, or

(e) by reason of the Architect's instructions issued under clauses 1 (2), 11 (1) or 21 (2) of these Conditions, or

(f) by reason of the Contractor not having received in due time necessary instructions, drawings, details or levels from the Architect for which he specially applied in writing on a date which having regard to the Date of Completion stated in the appendix to these Conditions or to any extension of time then fixed under this clause or clause 33 (1) (c) of these Conditions was neither unreasonably distant from nor unreasonably close to the date on which it was necessary for him to receive the same, or

(g) by delay on the part of nominated sub-contractors or nominated suppliers which the Contractor has taken all practicable steps to avoid or reduce, or

(h) by delay on the part of the artists, tradesmen or others engaged by the Employer in executing work not forming part of this Contract, or

(i) by reason of the opening up for inspection of any work covered up or of the testing of any of the work materials or goods in accordance with clause 6 (3) [45] of these Conditions (including making good in consequence of such opening or testing) unless the inspection or test showed that the work materials or goods were not in accordance with this Contract, or

(j) [46] (i) by the Contractor's inability for reasons beyond his control and which he could not reasonably have foreseen at the date of this Contract to secure such

---

[45] Which authorises the architect to require the contractor to open up any work.
[46] A footnote in the form of contract provides for either or both of the sub-paragraphs under (j) to be deleted if not to apply.

labour as is essential to the proper carrying out of the Works, or

(ii) by the Contractor's inability for reasons beyond his control and which he could not reasonably have foreseen at the date of this Contract to secure such goods and/or materials as are essential to the proper carrying out of the Works, or

(k) by reason of compliance with the provisions of clause 34 [47] or with Architect's instructions issued thereunder,

then the Architect shall . . . make in writing a fair and reasonable extension of time for completion of the Works. . . .

I.C.E., clause 44.   Should the amount of extra or additional work of any kind, or other special circumstances of any kind whatsoever which may occur, be such as fairly to entitle the Contractor to an extension of time for the completion of the work, the Engineer shall determine the amount of such extension.   Provided the Engineer is not bound to take into account any extra or additional work or other circumstances unless the Contractor has within 28 days after such work has been commenced or such circumstances have arisen or as soon thereafter as it is practicable delivered to the Engineer full and detailed particulars of any claim to extension of time to which he may consider himself entitled in order that such claim may be investigated at the time.

I.Mech.E./I.E.E., clause 24.   If after the acceptance of the Tender, by reason of any industrial dispute or any cause beyond the reasonable control of the Contractor, the Contractor shall have been delayed or impeded in the completion of the Works, whether such delay or impediment occur before or after the time (if any) or extended time fixed for Completion, provided that the Contractor shall without delay have given to the Employer or the Engineer notice in writing of his claim for an extension of time, the Engineer shall on receipt of such notice grant the Contractor from time to time either prospectively or retrospectively such extension of the time fixed by the Contract for the completion of the Works as may be reasonable.

[47] Which deals with the action to be taken in respect of any antiquities or objects of interest or value found in the course of the work.

Although these clauses differ in their wording, their effect is broadly the same. It is for the contractor to take the initiative by applying for an extension, whereupon the architect or engineer is under obligation to grant such extension as is reasonably justified by the facts. In this the three types of contract are reasonably drawn, but it is important for the contractor to remember that the initiative is his and not to assume that this escape mechanism operates automatically. There is a tendency for those in charge of construction contracts to assume that the extension of time for conditions of *force majeure* is automatic in the sense that the *force majeure* can be called in aid subsequently as an excuse for late completion. The fact that the relations between the architect or engineer, on the one hand, and the contractor, on the other, have been friendly and informal can cause the proper formalities to be overlooked. This should not be allowed to happen.

A more stringent type of clause is sometimes found in contracts entered into with foreign employers, in which it is required of the contractor that he gives formal notification of the happening of the event constituting the *force majeure* within a specified number of days of its occurrence. Sometimes the clause calls for the filing of documents certifying the existence of the state of *force majeure*, in which event it may be necessary to obtain from a recognised Chamber of Commerce, or from the Board of Trade, a letter certifying the existence of a trade dispute or other happening which gives rise to a claim for extended time.

In each of the clauses quoted the extension of time is claimed in the circumstances described as a matter of right, and the architect or engineer is called upon to use his discretion only in estimating the reasonableness of the claim or in calculating the proper extension. It will frequently be found that where the conditions of contract are framed by or exclusively in the interest of the employer, the operation of the clause is entirely dependent upon the discretion of the consultant or even of the employer. Thus:

> If by any reason of any of the following . . . [here follow a number of the usual hazards recognised as *force majeure*] . . . the Contractors claim that they have been unduly delayed in the progress of their work they shall make written request to the Engineer for an extension of time for

completion of the work or any portion of it. Should the Engineer consider such claim to be valid, he shall recommend to the Board that they grant such extension of time as may seem to them to be reasonable without thereby prejudicing or in any manner affecting the validity of the Contract.[48]

This clause is open to two objections from the point of view of the contractor. First, it does not place the power to grant extensions of time in the hands of the engineer; all he can do is recommend. The clause does not even suggest that the engineer should recommend the length of the extension to be granted, although it is presumed that his advice in the matter would be received and would be given some weight. Secondly, it gives no *right* to the contractor to have any extension at all. It is a very long way from the fairness of the I.Mech.E./I.E.E. conditions which lay a duty on the engineer. " The Engineer shall . . . grant . . . such extension as may be reasonable." Since any extension depends upon the discretion of the employing authority, which, because of the existence of a conventional " penalty " clause in the same conditions has a direct financial interest in the decision, the clause is fundamentally unjust.

In practice, the contractor does well to avoid this kind of provision, especially in an overseas contract, because it is not safe to assume that other systems of law will regard a duty to act reasonably and fairly as implicit in such a contract. The decision is placed in the hands of one party to the contract and he is constituted judge in his own cause.

9. Liquidated damages

It is natural to pass from consideration of the obligation to complete the work to time to the subject of " liquidated damages " or, as they are more often called, " penalties." Each of the three common forms makes provision for this sanction against the contractor who defaults in the completion date, and most contracts which follow the same tradition and are modelled upon any of them do the same.

The obligation is laid upon the contractor to finish the work by a certain date. He has either specified the date himself or has acquiesced in its appointment by the employer or his

[48] Development Board of the Government of Iraq.

architect or engineer. He has been given the right to claim an extension in the event of delays due to *force majeure* and, if the architect or engineer has acted in accordance with the contract, the extension will be reasonable having regard to the circumstances complained of. There is no apparent reason, therefore, why the contractor should not finish at the proper time, and if he fails to do so he is in breach of his contract.

The remedy for breach of contract is damages. The aggrieved party may be able, in addition, if the contract is broken to claim that he is himself discharged from the obligations resting in him and can eject the contractor from the works and employ another contractor to finish the work. This would be done in practice only in the most extreme cases because the change of contractor would itself occasion serious delays and aggravate an already unsatisfactory position.

The concept of damages is a very simple one. It is that the party who has broken an agreement may be required to make good to the aggrieved party the financial loss he has suffered as a result of the breach, the essence of the theory being that the aggrieved party should be put into the same position as he would have enjoyed had the breach not occurred, in so far as this is possible of achievement by a money payment. It is clearly established that the measure (or quantum) of damages is assessable under two heads. The first is the damage " arising naturally," *i.e.* " according to the ordinary course of things " and the second " such as may reasonably be supposed to have been in the contemplation of both parties at the time they made the contract, as the probable result of the breach of it." In a more recent case [49] the principles laid down in *Hadley* v. *Baxendale* [50] were clearly considered and reinforced to make it clear that the court would include in the quantum of damages the financial loss which the aggrieved party has suffered as a result of loss of profits due to the non-completion or late completion of the contract, provided that these profits could be reasonably foreseen by the defaulting party as likely to arise from the use to which he could reasonably assume that the goods supplied or the works carried out under the contract would be put.

[49] *Victoria Laundry (Windsor)* v. *Newman Industries Coulson & Co. (Third Parties)* [1949] 2 K.B. 528.
[50] *Hadley* v. *Baxendale* (1854) 9 Ex. 341.

It is important for a proper consideration of the so-called penalty clause to realise just how severe the measure of damages could be towards a defaulting contractor who, having promised completion by a stated date, fails to meet his obligation. The measure of damages is related to the reasonably foreseeable consequence of default and bears no relation whatever to the magnitude of the subject-matter of the contract. This must be underlined because the emphasis which, in English law, is placed on the concept of reasonableness can lead to misapprehension in the minds of businessmen, who assume that because a course of action appears to them to lead to a result unreasonable to them, it will not be upheld by the courts. Their mistake is due to their failure to see the same facts from the point of view of the other party to the contract. A principle of every system of law, indeed, the basis upon which alone it is possible for any system of law to work, is *pacta sunt servanda* – promises are to be kept. If the failure to supply an article upon the date for which it has been promised foreseeably involves the intended recipient in the loss of a thousand pounds, it is no answer to argue that because the default concerned only the non-delivery of an article worth much less it is not " reasonable " to visit so heavy a loss upon the default.

If, therefore, a contract is so worded as to make it possible that " damages at large " (*i.e.* damages calculated according to the common law rules) can be claimed, there is no actual or theoretical limit to the liability of the defaulting party. Certainly there is none that can be calculated with any accuracy. For this reason the almost invariable inclusion of a " penalty clause " is an advantage to both sides in a construction contract and, if the truth be told, is really of more value to the contractor than to the employer. In our common form contracts the provision appears in terms which are broadly similar but which exhibit differences of sufficient interest to justify their quotation in full.

R.I.B.A., clause 22. If the Contractor fails to complete the Works by the Date for Completion stated in the appendix to these Conditions or within any extended time fixed under clause 23 or clause 33 (1) (c) of these Conditions and the Architect certifies in writing that in his opinion the same ought reasonably so to have been completed, then the Contractor

H

shall pay or allow to the Employer a sum calculated at the rate stated in the said appendix as Liquidated and Ascertained Damages for the period during which the Works shall so remain or have remained incomplete, and the Employer may deduct any such sum from any monies due or to become due to the Contractor under this Contract.

I.C.E., clause 47 (1). If the Contractor shall fail to complete the Works within the time prescribed by clause 43 hereof or extended time then the Contractor shall pay to the Employer the sum stated in the Tender as liquidated damages for such default and not as a penalty for every week or part of a week which shall elapse between the time prescribed by clause 43 hereof or extended time as the case may be and the date of completion of the Works. The Employer may without prejudice to any other method of recovery deduct the amount of such damage from any monies in his hands due or which may become due to the Contractor. The payment or deduction of such damages shall not relieve the Contractor from his obligation to complete the Works or from any other of his obligations and liabilities under the Contract.

I.Mech.E./I.E.E., clause 25. If the Contractor fail to complete the Works in accordance with the Contract (except the maintenance thereof as provided in clause 29 and such tests as are to be made in accordance with clause 26) within the time fixed by the Contract for the completion of the Works or any extension of such time, or if no time be fixed, within a reasonable time, and the Purchaser shall have suffered any loss from such failure, there shall be deducted from the Contract Price the percentage named in the Appendix of the Contract value of such portions only of the Works as cannot in consequence of the said failure be put to the use intended for each week between the time for completion of the Works as aforesaid and the actual date of completion, but the amount so deducted shall not in any case exceed the maximum percentage named in the Appendix of the Contract value of such portion or portions of the Works, and such deduction shall be in full satisfaction of the Contractor's liability for the said failure.

CONTRACTS FOR BUILDING, ETC.

Before commenting upon these clauses it should be noted that the meaning of " liquidate " in this context is " make clear," and the essence of the idea of liquidated damages is that the parties have agreed between themselves at the time of entering into the contract what method will be used to measure the damages in the case of delay in completion.

It will be noted that in the R.I.B.A. contract a subjective element on the part of the architect is imported: " the Architect certifies that *in his opinion the same ought* reasonably to have been completed." By what criteria the word " ought " should be interpreted is left undefined. The words must, however, operate to the advantage of the contractor because a sympathetic architect can relieve him of liability but cannot increase it. The appendix, however, provides for a daily rate of damages but for no maximum. The I.C.E. contract omits any such reference to the opinion of the engineer, and, like the R.I.B.A. contract, makes no provision in the " Form of Tender " annexed to the conditions for a maximum. The I.Mech.E./I.E.E. contract, like the I.C.E., does not include any subjective test based upon the opinion of the engineer as to whether the works " ought " to have been completed, but introduces a new and important factor in the words " and the Purchaser shall have suffered any loss from such failure," and the Appendix does provide a line for the maximum damages to be prescribed. These differences, though small, are important, and the I.Mech.E./I.E.E. conditions are, from the point of view of the contractor, the most favourable. The contractor operating under the other conditions or similar conditions involving a daily, weekly or monthly rate of liquidated damages without prescribing a maximum, is well advised to insist upon the inclusion of such a maximum.

All elementary textbooks of contract law draw the attention of the student to the fact that in English law a " penalty " will not be enforced, and in drawing a distinction between " penalty " and " liquidated damages " they rightly emphasise that the question whether a sum of this kind chargeable against the contractor is in fact a penalty or liquidated damages is one which will not be answered by what it is called, *i.e.* one does not make a penalty enforceable merely by calling it liquidated damages. The distinction is, however, so well known that the word " penalty " has dropped out of English contracts, though fixed just as firmly as ever in the vocabulary of contractors. The fact that the penalty as such is not enforceable has led to a very general feeling in the minds of contractors in the United Kingdom that this type of clause will only be enforced in very extreme circumstances. There is a feeling that it stands as a warning of what may happen if a contractor is very seriously at fault, rather than as an indication of what will happen if he does not maintain his scheduled dates. This generalisation may have some truth, but it should be remembered that it has no legal ground whatever, that other systems of law do not share the English objection to " penalities " as such, and that employing authorities in other countries do not show any tenderness in using the provisions of a penalty clause to reduce the cost of a contract to them.

The tests to be applied in order to ascertain whether a provision of this kind is a penalty or liquidated damages were reviewed by Lord Dunedin in *Dunlop Pneumatic Tyre Co.* v. *New Garage Co. Ltd.*[51] In summarised form they can be presented thus:

(a) The expression used, whether " penalty " or " damages " is not conclusive, although prima facie the parties may be presumed to mean what they say.

(b) The essential nature of a penalty is that it is stipulated *in terrorem* of the offending party: of liquidated damages is that it is a genuine pre-estimate of the damage likely to be suffered.

(c) Which of the two clauses a stipulation falls into must be decided according to the construction of the contract and in the light of circumstances existing at the time the contract was made.

(d) The stipulation will be a penalty if:

   (i) the sum is extravagant or unreasonable in comparison with the greatest loss that could flow from the breach.

   (ii) Presumptively (but not conclusively) if a single lump sum is made payable upon the happening of one or all of several events, some of which may occasion serious and others but trifling damage.

(e) A sum may be a genuine pre-estimate of damages, even though any precise pre-estimation is impossible.

[51] [1915] A.C. 79 at p. 86 (H.L.).

The kind of clause which has become familiar in constructional contracts in the United Kingdom falls fairly clearly within the class of liquidated damages, and only rarely is it likely to be possible for it to be set aside as a penalty and therefore unenforceable. It is to be noted that to attempt to set it aside in this way could be against the contractor's interests, because the obligation to pay liquidated damages cannot be removed without removing the limit which it imposes upon the contractor's liabilities and exposing him to a claim for damages at large. Generally speaking, only if the contractor is prepared to argue that the aggrieved employer suffered no loss from his lateness would such an exercise be in his interest.

In some foreign contracts a form of words will be found which renders the right of the employer to claim a penalty on the basis of a stated percentage for each week of delay to be without prejudice to his right to recover the actual damage suffered. Such a clause is not often found in English contracts because the penalty, whether described as such or designated " liquidated damages," would be clearly a mere penalty and therefore unenforceable. A clause of this kind is manifestly most inequitable and should be resisted.

When a main contractor is faced with a liquidated damages clause, which by percentage is related to the whole contract sum, but is dependent for the fulfilment of his obligations upon a number of sub-contractors, whose contracts are much smaller in size, a difficult problem can arise. It is clear that if the sub-contractor enters into a commitment to complete his section of the work by a stated time in the knowledge that if he fails the main contractor may be involved in payment of liquidated damages on the whole contract, then, in the absence of any provision to the contrary, he will be liable under the rules of *Hadley* v. *Baxendale* [52] to indemnify the main contractor in full. Comment has already been made [53] upon the onerous provisions which have been inserted in the standard form of sub-contract " Issued under the sanction of and approved by the National Federation of Building Trades Employers and the Federation of Associations of Specialists and Sub-Contractors." The clause reads as follows:

[52] (1854) 9 Ex. 341.
[53] pp. 73–74.

> If the Sub-contractor fails to complete the Sub-contract works or any section thereof within the period specified or any extended period as hereinafter provided, he shall pay to the Contractor *any loss or damage suffered or incurred by the Contractor* and caused by the failure of the Sub-contractor as aforesaid of which loss or damage the Contractor shall at the earliest opportunity give reasonable notice to the Sub-contractor that the same is being or has been suffered or incurred.[54]

That a sub-contract is available in standard printed form embodying these words shows that the obligation is frequently accepted by sub-contractors, but it is doubtful if it would be readily accepted if its harshness were recognised. It goes, in fact, farther than the common law principles concerning damages at large under the two rules in *Hadley* v. *Baxendale*[55] since the words italicised appear to seek to involve the sub-contractor in damage suffered by the main contractor which might not have been reasonably contemplated by the parties at the time the contract was entered into.

Since the situation in which specialist sub-contractors are employed is typically one in which the sub-contract is one of many undertaken in parallel by a variety of sub-contractors, it is disappointing to find that this standard form of contract does not give any indication of the method to be used to apportion liability if more than one sub-contractor is late. Since they may be working side by side, and to a considerable degree operate in mutual dependence, the cumulative lateness may not equal the sum of their individual lateness, and indeed will hardly ever do so. For example, if the main contractor is ten weeks late in handing over a complete building, contributory factors being that the lighting sub-contractor, the flooring sub-contractor and the lift installation sub-contractor were all in default to the same approximate extent, which of the three " caused " the loss to the main contractor? It is curious that a form of contract agreed between professional societies should fail to be adequate to deal with a simple practical situation of this kind, one often met with. Indeed, it gives the impression of having been drawn without reference to practical

---

[54] Cl. 8 (a) of Standard Form of Sub-contract.
[55] p. 96.

realities of the industry and on the basis of a purely legal approach to a hypothetical situation.

Another aspect of the difficulties posed by this treatment derives from the fact that the consequences of default could be so out of proportion with the magnitude of a sub-contract that no sub-contractor in his senses would accept the obligation if he clearly envisaged what it could mean. If a total scheme which is the subject of an overall liquidated damages clause at the rate of $\frac{1}{2}$ per cent. per week is worth £1,000,000 it would be folly for a sub-contractor whose proportion of the works is worth only £10,000 to accept this form of sub-contract, since if he is only a fortnight late and can be shown to have been the cause of the lateness of completion of the whole scheme by this period he will receive no payment at all for his work, the main contractor being liable for one per cent. or £10,000 by way of liquidated damages.

There is probably no completely fair solution of the problem how to apportion any amount suffered in the form of liquidated damages by a main contractor between that contractor and one or more sub-contractors who are themselves responsible for the delay in varying degrees. This being so, it is important that the problem be clearly faced at the time when sub-contracts are placed, and clearly expressed in those sub-contracts. One method is for an arbitrary figure to be placed upon each sub-contract as the appropriate liquidated damages for each week's delay on his part, the figure being adjusted to each sub-contractor so as not to be completely unreasonable in relation to the size of the sub-contract. This method is, however, open to the objection that if, as has been laid down, it is evident that a stipulation for payment is a penalty if the same sum is applied to different degrees of damage, it might be held by analogy (although the point does not yet appear to have been considered by the courts) that if a different sum is predicated in different sub-contracts for default which must involve identical damage to the main contractor, those sums cannot be a genuine pre-estimate of damage and are therefore of the nature of a penalty and unenforceable.

An entirely different approach is for the sub-contractor to be made subject to an obligation of the same kind but larger in proportion than that contained in the main contract. Thus, if the main contractor is subject to liquidated damages on the basis of

½ per cent. per week with a maximum of ten per cent. the sub-contractor may be made subject on a scale of one per cent. per week with a maximum of twenty per cent. or twenty-five per cent. In the event of delay occurring the amount recovered by the main contractor from the sub-contractor will go some way towards recouping his own obligation. To the extent that it does not do so he can be regarded as bearing the commercial risks inherent in being a main contractor, who, after all, does take a profit on all the sub-contractor's charges. It may be possible for this risk to be made the subject of insurance in some circumstances, for although it is not normally possible to insure against the consequences of one's own contractual default, it is not impossible to insure against the consequences of default by another party. Such insurance would, however, call for a specially negotiated cover, and it would be necessary to write a policy around the actual circumstances of the case.

Because the inclusion of " penalty " provisions in contracts was regarded as contrary to the public interest, the courts, specially through the nineteenth century when many of the present building precedents were established, have tended to look narrowly on the application of these clauses even where the sanction is defensible as truly " liquidated damages." To enforce such a clause is sometimes difficult if the contractor can show that any part of his apparent default was due to a failure on the part of the employer or the consultant. This attitude on the part of the courts has led to an unspoken assumption in the minds of many " practical " people that it is generally possible to argue one's way out of the consequences of " penalty clauses." Such an attitude is unwise for two very good reasons. The first is simply that the assumption is unsound. The second is that if a liquidated damages clause is applied it is generally by withholding payment, so that the initiative in litigation will have to be taken by the contractor claiming the money, when the clause will be claimed as applicable by the defence. This to the contractor is a far less satisfactory situation tactically than one in which application of the clause is sought by a plaintiff.

10. Sureties and guarantees

The I.Mech.E./I.E.E. conditions and those of the I.C.E. contain

provisions for the contractor to provide sureties for the due performance of the contract. No such provision is contained in the
standard R.I.B.A. document. None of the three common form
documents used in this section calls for a tender guarantee or,
as the Americans call it, a "bid bond." The two classes of
guarantee are so commonly called for, however, especially in
respect of foreign tenders and contracts, that they may well be
considered together.

A surety is one who promises to be answerable for the
"debt default or miscarriage" of another. The document by
which he gives the promise is executed under seal since no
consideration moves to him from the promisee in respect of his
promise.[56] It is therefore called a "bond," this word denoting
a solemn promise given under seal. In form a bond is a "promise
defeasible upon condition subsequent," which is to say that it is
an unqualified promise to pay a sum of money, subject to the
condition that if a certain event happens then the promise will
be of no effect. The event which defeats the promise in cases
like this is the fulfilment of the contractor's obligations under the
contract. The following is a form of bond used in conjunction
with the I.C.E. contract (slightly abridged):

> By this Bond, we, (the Contractor) and (the Surety) are
> held and firmly bound unto (the Employer) in the sum of
> — pounds for the payment of which sum the Contractor
> and the Surety bind themselves their successors and assigns
> jointly and severally by these presents.
>
> Whereas the Contractor . . . has entered into a contract
> (with the Employer) for the construction completion and
> maintenance of certain works, etc. . . .
>
> Now the Condition of the above written Bond is such
> that if the Contractor shall duly perform and observe all
> the terms provisions conditions and stipulations of the said
> contract . . . then this obligation shall be null and void
> but otherwise shall be and remain in full force and effect,
> etc. . . .

It will be observed that in this case the bond is entered into
by the contractor as well as the surety or sureties. The form

---

[56] For an explanation of this point, reference may be made to any standard
textbook on the law of contract.

used in the I.Mech.E./I.E.E. contract is designated a guarantee, and is prepared for execution by the surety only. Where the contractor is a company it is not unusual for one or more of its directors to act as sureties, and they are likely in turn to be indemnified by the company within the terms of their service agreements, if any. If they have no express indemnity in this way they will still be indemnified by common law principles and also, in many instances, by the Articles of Association of the Company.

Where bonds are given by sureties or guarantors under English law the courts will enforce them only to the extent that the employer, in whose favour they are given, can show that he has suffered loss by the default of the contractor.[57] The bond or guarantee therefore operates as little more than evidence of the existence and answerability of some person or corporation (since it is not unusual for the surety or guarantor to be a bank or insurance company and, indeed, some employers insist upon this) upon whom the burden of damages will fall in the event of the contractor being in default and insolvent. It must not be overlooked, however, that other systems of law may not be so tender in their approach to the matter.

In the case of overseas contracts the procedure is usually different. In home contracts the employer and the contractor are within a common jurisdiction, and if there is default on the part of the contractor there is no difficulty in the employer's suing him and making judgment effective, so that the bond may be safely taken from the contractor or its directors. Where the employer is in a foreign country, however, he calls for a bank guarantee, because he wishes to be certain that in the event of default there will be some party within his own country to whom he can go for compensation. The procedure will then be based on a bank guarantee, and frequently in addition the practice of taking a " bid bond " is introduced. In such cases instead of a personal bond being given by an individual the undertaking to make payment is given by a bank in the territory of the employer, which will be instructed and indemnified by the contractor's own bank, which in turn will take a counter-indemnity from the contractor himself. No money will actually pass, except for the

[57] *Workington Harbour and Dock Board* v. *Trade Indemnity Co. Ltd.* (*No.* 2) [1938] 2 All E.R. 101.

payment of commission and charges, unless and until the employer invokes the guarantee, but to enter into such an arrangement involves a contingent liability on the part of the contractor.

The terms of the contract will usually provide that if the tender is accepted and the contract awarded to the contractor the " bid bond " or " tender guarantee " will be increased in amount and converted into a " performance " bond or guarantee, whose effect will be substantially the same as the bond entered into by the surety under the home contract.

Both in the bid bond and the performance bond there is a promise to pay, defeasible upon the happening of a stated event. In the case of the bid bond the payment is relatively small, and the event is the signing of the contract; in the case of the performance bond the payment is larger and the event is the completion of the contract. As to the magnitude of the amounts, one per cent. or two per cent. of the contract sum is usual for a bid bond, and five to fifteen per cent. for a performance bond. Larger figures than this are frequently met with, but should be regarded as unreasonable and resisted if possible. In general terms it may be said that the reasonable amount for a performance bond is the amount of the retention money, which is to say that portion of the contract price which is paid only at the end of the period for which the contractor is required under the contract to maintain the works. Thus, if the terms of payment are:

Ten per cent. on the signing of the contract

Sixty per cent. by instalments against certificates during the progress of the works

Twenty per cent. on completion

Ten per cent. after six months, during which the works are to be maintained by the contractor,

the appropriate amount of the performance bond would be ten per cent. and a claim for a larger bond than this should be resisted, especially if it is demanded as a bank guarantee.

The purpose inherent in this machinery is the protection of the employer against default by the contractor, whom it would be difficult for the employer to sue owing to his being outside the jurisdiction of the employer's country. The " bid bond " is forfeit if, upon being offered a contract on the basis of his tender, the tenderer refuses to enter upon the contract. It therefore operates as a sanction against the possible submission of frivolous tenders. In consequence, a bid bond should never be given unless all the details of the proposed contract are known to be acceptable, since it may subsequently be impossible to contest any conditions without forfeiting the bond. The performance bond is forfeit in the event of failure to carry out the contract according to the terms. They follow a regular pattern, and the machinery of their establishment and operation is well understood by the banks. It is not always realised, however, how categorical they are, considered as undertakings to pay, and to what extent the contractor, setting up such a guarantee, has placed himself at the mercy of the employer. If the employer draws on the credit fraudulently or unjustifiably the only remedy of the contractor is to sue the employer in the courts of the employer's own country. The following is typical of the wording used in these guarantees:

> We, the undersigned — whose registered office is situated at — have financially guaranteed Messrs. — Contractors to Contract No. — bearing even date to this letter, to the amount of —.
>
> We undertake to pay you the said amount at your first demand without warning or any restriction or other condition, and the said amount shall be at your disposal from the date of issue of this Bank Guarantee until the — day of — 19—, i.e. — months after guaranteed time limit for completion of works or until such extended date as may be necessary to cover the entire Period of Guarantee, unless you were to cancel the present Bank Guarantee before the end of the period of Guarantee.
>
> All demands not presented to this Bank within the above-mentioned dates shall be considered null and cancelled.[58]

It is hardly necessary to point out that in permitting an overseas bank to issue such a guarantee on the basis of ultimate reliance upon a counter-indemnity given by himself, the contractor manifests a high degree of confidence in the good faith of the employer, and it is gratifying to note that although many such guarantees are given, only rarely are they abused. In addition to the banks this type of operation is also undertaken by insurance companies and by some specialist undertakings amongst the

[58] Form of Bond put forward by Ministry of Industry, Republic of Iraq.

merchant banks. They do not, however, make it their practice to underwrite the risk of the guarantee being misused and the guaranteed sum being wrongly seized by the employer.

11. Certificates for payment

It is usual in constructional contracts carried out under the supervision of an architect or engineer for the contractor to be paid in accordance with certificates issued by him. There is some variation in the detailed arrangements provided in the three common form contracts used as a basis of this chapter, and still more variations when one goes beyond them into the individual variants offered. The R.I.B.A. provide for a regular (*e.g.* monthly) certification, the I.C.E. stipulates monthly certification as the norm, and the I.Mech.E./I.E.E. provides that the contractor shall make application " from time to time." In each case the form of the contract lays upon the architect or engineer the obligation to issue the certificate. To some degree his estimation of the amount may be subjective, in the sense that it will be affected by his opinion regarding the completeness and satisfactory quality of sections of the work, but in the main the criteria by which his decision is taken are objective, consisting of the value of the work done and the value of materials brought on to the site, which under the vesting clause will have become the property of the employer under the contract. In his supervision and direction of the work the architect or engineer acts as the agent of the employer, but it is in respect of the issue of certificates that the principle of his position as an arbitrator standing fairly and disinterestedly between the parties has been emphasised in the judgments already referred to. In the leading case [59] the architect withheld his certificate under pressure from the employer and upon being pressed by the contractor wrote to the effect that he " had . . . better call and see my client because in the face of their instructions to me I cannot issue a certificate whatever my own private opinion in the matter." It was made abundantly clear in the course of the judgment that, in subordinating his power to issue a certificate in accordance with the facts and his own conscience, he had lost his independence. It remains true and worthy of note, however, that judgment was given against the

[59] *Hickman & Co.* v. *Roberts* [1913] A.C. 229 (H.L.).

employer and not against the architect, illustrating the principle that the consultant is not himself a party to the agreement, notwithstanding that it purports to lay duties upon him.

In the case of contracts for the erection of machinery it is not unusual for the appropriate points in time for the issue of certificates and the making of payments to be related to the delivery of the whole of the plant to the site and subsequently the completion of erection. The R.I.B.A. speaks of " practical completion," the I.C.E. of " substantial completion," whilst the I.Mech.E./I.E.E. is more extensive:

> As soon as the Works have been completed in accordance with the contract (except in minor respects that do not affect their use for the purpose for which they are intended . . .) the Engineer shall issue a certificate. . . .

The principle is the same. It is a simple fact that many building or engineering contracts never reach a point at which diligent search could not find something which still needs to be done, and an unreasonable attitude in this regard by the consultant can involve delays which are very costly to the contractor. It is possible for an unreasonably exacting attitude to lead to such delays in the issue of completion certificates that normal wear and tear becomes confused with and treated as constituting defects in completion. Thus, the principle *de minimis non curat lex* is not left to be invoked by inference but finds express embodiment in the contract. It must, however, be admitted that whilst the course of dealing between the contractor and consultant is normally smooth and reasonable, where any tendency to small-mindedness becomes evident, it is possible for a consultant to adopt a legalistic attitude and by so doing to involve a contractor in very considerable expense.

The duty of consultants in respect of certification, which in the *Hickman & Co.* v. *Roberts* [60] judgment is made abundantly clear as regards principle and practice in the United Kingdom, can also be complicated in some overseas countries, especially where the employer is itself a government organ, by government interference with the freedom of the consultant. The author's own experience includes an instance in which the government of a foreign country, a department of which was party to an entirely

[60] p. 109.

conventional engineering contract passed a " Ministerial Order " which effectively removed from its own consultant any power to certify payments and instead vested the power in its own technical committee. The effect was to keep contractors waiting for their money literally for years. It must not be overlooked that law and justice are not synonymous. Law is what the legislature of any country makes it. The best and only safeguard which the contractor can look for is a longstanding tradition of independence of the judiciary and a record of fair dealing. In going into countries where these cannot be found the contractor faces hazards. He does so and must continue to do so in the knowledge that his overseas contracts constitute no small part of the export trade upon which the life of an industrial country largely depends.

CHAPTER 4

PRICE VARIATION IN CONTRACTS

ONE problem which constantly faces the manufacturer of those products which are custom made and which consume time in the making, as it does even more the contractor concerned with building, civil engineering and the like, is that of price variations. It would be relatively simple to calculate the cost of making the article, whether it be a piece of electrical switchgear, a chemical plant or a ship, if one could only be sure that the cost of raw materials, of manufactured components, of labour, and of social security and other taxes would remain unchanged. But they do not. The buyer always presses for a firm price that will not be subject to any variation, the seller tends, especially in a period which is recognisably one of inflationary pressures, to be cautious, and tries to protect himself.

The history of the handling of this problem by the use of what are called " price ruling " clauses, or " rise and fall " or " escalation " clauses is an interesting one from which something can be learned. The matter became acute at the end of the 1939–45 war, when demand, especially for engineering products, buildings and capital goods, outstripped supply so grossly that delivery periods ran into years and when the buyer was willing to accept almost any conditions merely to have his order accepted and to join the queue. Almost every article which could be regarded as having a recognisable market price, as for example if it figured in a published catalogue, if its dispatch was likely to be delayed by more than a few months from the placing of the order, would be sold subject to a clause added to the standard conditions saying something like:

> " Notwithstanding anything stated in our tender the goods will be invoiced at the prices ruling at the date of dispatch."

Where there was no identifiable ruling, a price variation clause would be imposed. This would be related if possible to officially published index figures, one for materials and one for wages, and the Board of Trade organised a series of materials indices for

the purpose. One much used formula related the ultimate contract price to the customer by selecting a date two-thirds of the
way from the date of tender to the date of delivery, and by
providing that for every one per cent. rise or fall in the index
relating to materials between the date of tender and the " reference
date " the price would be varied by 0·45 per cent., and for every
one per cent. rise or fall in the nationally negotiated rate of
wages for a specified grade of labour, by 0·40 per cent., with the
proviso that if the wage rate varied during the last third of the
period the modification would be made rateably to the proportion
of that one-third for which the wage variation applied. Each
industry tended to adopt its own formula.

These formulae, of course, always provided for the possibility
of a price reduction as well as of a price increase, but this rarely,
if ever, happened in practice. The mathematically calculable
price variation formula was regarded by buyers, especially those
of public authorities, as better than " price ruling " clauses,
because these, it was sometimes thought, were tantamount to
signing a blank cheque in favour of the seller. For about five
years or so, however, the position held and a sellers' market
continued. Then the situation imperceptibly changed. Sellers
began to experience competition, and price variation was a
bargaining point. They began to lengthen the periods within
which they would not seek variation and would themselves take
the risk of fluctuation in costs. From the early 'fifties to the
nineteen-sixties this continued until by the middle 'sixties price
variation clauses were rare.

Then came a new wave of inflation following upon devaluation
in 1968. Many major undertakings faced soaring wage and
material costs without the protection of the old clauses, which
had fallen into almost complete disuse after the passing of the
Restrictive Trade Practices Act 1956 effectively removed the tight
control formerly exercised over their members by some trade
associations. It is no secret that the disastrous situation in which
many large organisations such as Rolls-Royce and Upper Clyde
Shipbuilders were to be found was to a large degree due to
their having accepted major contracts without the protection of
price variation clauses. In consequence, there has been a renewal
of interest in this type of clause, and although official policy makes
it difficult to persuade buyers for public authorities to accept them

– they prefer a price loaded against this contingency – there is a renewed demand for them by manufacturers and contractors.

These clauses come in all shapes and sizes. It is sufficient to point out that they are basically divided into four kinds. The first is the " price ruling " type, where the customer is required to accept the goods at whatever price is " ruling " when the goods are dispatched. This is most commonly used for relatively standard articles, such as motor cars. The second is the rise and fall clause, embodying a formula related to publicly accessible indices. This may well be used for a major engineering product that is custom built. The third is used when the product is so predominantly based upon a single commodity that the manufacturer is willing to carry the risk on all other manufacturing costs if he can be protected against fluctuation in this one product. It is the custom for sales of electric cable to be protected against copper fluctuations as evidenced by the London Metal Exchange price. The fourth is a protection designed to give the contractor his actual increase of costs because of fluctuations, no more and no less. The long optional clause included in the Institution of Civil Engineers model contract is an example of this.

CHAPTER 5

THE CARRIAGE OF GOODS

1. In home trade

THERE is at once a similarity and a difference between the contract for the carriage of goods and that for the sale of goods; similarity in that it is possible to establish a " norm " which is itself rooted in the common law and statute, difference in that the deviation from that norm, through the medium of printed conditions, tends to be a one-sided affair.   In the last three chapters it was evident that both in respect of the sale of goods and the erection of buildings or machinery there is a tug-of-war or battle of wits between the seller and the buyer in which the result depends largely upon their relative economic strength.   The same struggle can, of course, occur in respect of the carriage of goods, but in practice the available common form conditions of carriage are drawn up by the carrier and not by the consignor or consignee. Sometimes the relationship between the carrier and the consignor is close enough and the traffic to be placed with the carrier significant enough for the economic strength of the consignor to be brought to bear and a special contract prepared.   For the most part, however, both consignors and consignees tend to take conditions of carriage as they find them.   When the consignor reaches a position of dominance in which he might be in a position to dictate conditions of carriage his line of action is more likely to be in the direction of owning and operating his own transport.

The history of the contract for the carriage of goods is a long one.   The principal statute relating to it is the Carriers Act 1830, which antedated the opening up of the railway systems of the country, and this measure itself modified rather than codified a law which had already emerged through the practice of merchants and carriers and had crystallised in the judgments of the courts.   In retrospect there could hardly have been a more inopportune moment for even a partial codification of the law, for it was on September 15, 1830 that the Liverpool and Manchester Railway was opened, the first major railway project to come into public service, and within ten years the entire picture of inland transport had changed beyond recognition.

It will be found that in any academic study of the contract of carriage a good deal of attention is given to the distinction between the " common carrier " and the " private carrier." The " common carrier " is one who makes carrying his business, who " holds himself out to the world as prepared for hire to transport from place to place the goods of any person wishing to employ him, while a man who undertakes to carry goods for certain persons is not a common, but a ' private ' carrier." [1] Traditionally, the essential difference in the nature of the contract made with a common carrier and that made with a private carrier was the degree of liability accepted by each in respect of loss or damage to the goods entrusted to him. The common carrier accepted an absolute liability and stood in the position of an insurer of the goods, subject to the protection given by the Carriers Act in regard to certain articles of special value.[2] The liability of the private carrier was limited to loss or damage attributable to his negligence or that of his servants.

A number of circumstances have led to the virtual disappearance of the " common carrier " in the legal sense of the expression, so that the distinction is no longer of significance. First, it was always possible for a carrier to modify his liabilities by special terms of contract and, following the same pattern as has been evident in the case of the sale of goods, the tradition has been followed of writing conditions and seeking to apply them by unobtrusive notices so that the knowledge of the conditions could be attributed to the other party without his being deliberately alerted. To be within the category of a common carrier carried little or no advantage to the carrier to compensate for his special responsibility, and there was therefore every incentive for him to take advantage of the possibility of escaping from that responsibility. Secondly, as the nineteenth century progressed the carriage

---

[1] Kahn-Freund, *The Law of Carriage by Inland Transport* (4th ed. 1965), p. 196.
[2] This provision illustrates the manner in which the passing of time makes nonsense of provisions which, built into an Act of Parliament, remain unchanged because of the formality needed to alter them. The protection of the Act to the carrier consists in the requirement that in respect of certain types of article the carrier's liability is conditional upon the consignor declaring the nature and value of the articles if their value in one parcel exceeds £10. In 1830 this was a significant sum, representing the wages of a labourer for several months. It has never been altered, although the corresponding sum in the Railway Conditions is now £25.

of goods for the public passed to an increasing degree into the hands of the railway companies, and the attempts of these companies to avoid their liabilities as common carriers, coupled with their monopoly position, led to their being the subject of special legislation in a series of Acts, so that the conditions under which they carry goods became increasingly, and are now, entirely statute-based. Thirdly, and perhaps most significantly, is the fact that to be a common carrier it is necessary to come within the definition that a carrier " holds himself out to the world as prepared . . . to transport the goods of any person." The potential responsibilities of the common carrier being what they are, even though in practice and in fact he presents himself as ready to carry for any person, and indeed is active to solicit business from all and sundry, he will ensure that he does not so " hold himself out." He does this by the inclusion in his conditions of carriage of a clause expressly denying that he is a common carrier. Thus it is possible for a contemporary commentator on the law of inland transport to comment:

> At the present moment the old common carrier's liability is of very small importance. The Commission carries goods by rail under statutory conditions and road hauliers are, as a rule, private carriers. The common carrier's absolute liability, established for the protection of the public in the seventeenth and eighteenth centuries has to a large extent ceased to be part of the living law, and becomes a historical relic and textbook affair." [3]

The history of the past few decades has led to a special situation in respect of carriage by road as well as by rail, in that the nationalisation of road haulage under the Transport Act 1947, and its subsequent partial denationalisation under the Transport Act 1953, left the British Transport Commission as the most important road haulage undertaking in the country, whilst the tendency has been for the denationalised portion of road haulage business to be in the hands of undertakings which have provided themselves with standard conditions of carriage through their collaboration in the Road Haulage Association Ltd. The consignor of goods to inland destinations is therefore faced with three common form sets of conditions:

[3] Kahn-Freund, *op. cit.*

(a) The Railway Conditions based now upon the Transport Act which established a machinery for the preparation and approval of "Charge Schemes" under which a series of sets of conditions applicable to different types of traffic have been compiled.

(b) The standard conditions of British Road Services Ltd.

(c) The standard conditions of the Road Haulage Association Ltd. used and applied generally by its members.

As regards the last mentioned of these, however, there is a further complication. In April 1967 the Road Haulage Association introduced a new set of standard conditions. These follow very closely those of British Road Services and are more fairly drawn as between the consignor or consignee and the carrier than the 1961 conditions they replaced. But as a result of the Restrictive Trade Practices Act 1956 the power of trade associations to control the conditions of contract applied by their members has been limited, and many members of the Association continue to use the old conditions.

These documents manifest considerable differences. In the case of the Railway Conditions the standard booklet contains four sets of conditions, relating to general merchandise, livestock, coal and minerals, and goods carried by water. Each set of conditions is complete in itself. These four sets are not exhaustive, other specialised conditions being extant to apply to special merchandise. It is noticeable that although the Railway Conditions and those of the British Road Services are each the result of legal drafting on the part of departments of the former British Transport Commission, and although their general import is broadly similar, they present little similarity in draftsmanship and arrangement. Thus Condition 3 of the British Railways Board Conditions, dealing with transfer of goods to an independent carrier where this is necessary, is represented in the British Road Services Conditions by section 14, which though dealing with a similar situation is worded very differently. This dissimilarity in arrangements renders detailed comparison difficult, but the two sets of conditions have this in common, that each is designed to constitute a reasonably complete code of rules as between the carrier and the consignor, and is concerned to define rather than to deny liability on the part of the carrier. The same is true of the 1967 Conditions of the Road Haulage Association. The earlier (1961)

Conditions of the Road Haulage Association, however, were concerned almost exclusively with denying, excluding or limiting the liability of the carrier. This is not, of course, to say that the individual trader using the services of an individual carrier using these conditions would be subjected to less considerate treatment than he would experience if he were to use British Rail, British Road Services, or a private carrier using the new Road Haulage Association Conditions. It is simply an observation which can be verified by detailed comparisons of the sets of conditions, and will be illustrated by the examples quoted below.

The difference in approach is to some extent coloured by another consideration, that of the parallel " Company's Risk " and " Owner's Risk " concepts in railway conditions of carriage, which is rooted in the past and especially in the Railway and Canal Traffic Act 1854. The history of this Act is illuminating. During the twenty years from 1830 to 1850 the railways had become at first the principal and eventually the only major carriers in the country. Certainly, apart from the geographically limited facilities of canals, they possessed a virtual monopoly of all carriage of goods over distances exceeding those appropriate to horse-drawn traffic. Entrenched, as they were, in a monopoly position, they set to work to divest themselves of any liability for goods entrusted to them. The matter reached something of a scandal when it was found that even the consequences of gross negligence on the part of the employees of the railway could not be brought home to the companies because of the protection they had given themselves by a printed Conditions of Carriage.[4] In response to public agitation the Act of 1854 was passed. It laid upon the railway companies a positive duty to afford reasonable facilities for receiving, forwarding, and delivering traffic. The Act also provided [5] that railways were to be responsible for loss or injury to any goods entrusted to them, occasioned by their neglect or default or that of their servants, and further provided that any notice, condition, or declaration purporting to negative such liability should be null and void. This, if unqualified, would have fastened upon the railways most or all of the liabilities traditionally attached to the common carrier, but the Act entitled the railways, as an alternative to this full liability, to offer to the consignor

[4] *Carr* v. *Lancashire and Yorkshire Railway Co.* (1852) 7 Ex. 707.
[5] s. 7.

conditions which were "just and reasonable," provided that such
a contract were signed by the consignor or his agent. Some initial
ambiguities in the working of the Act led to uncertainties in
interpretation, but these were cleared up in 1863,[6] which made
it clear that it was necessary, in order for the railways to be
relieved of the full responsibility laid down in section 7 of the
1854 Act, for there to be a contract in writing and for it to be just
and reasonable, *i.e.* the overriding responsibility could be modified
only to an extent which it was "just and reasonable" to do. The
full responsibility of section 7 therefore constitutes the normal
contract for the carriage of goods, the modified liability now
generally recognised as "owner's risk" conditions grew up alongside the standard contract of carriage. The ruling of the House
of Lords in *Peek's* case [6] made it clear that:

(a) the railway was bound to carry under full liability
    for a reasonable charge, but

(b) could offer to carry at a lower rate with reduced
    liability, but the contract must still be fair and
    reasonable.

These rulings are now historical, since the 1854 Act was
repealed by the Transport Act 1962, but show how the two rates
arose. The independent carrier, now represented by the Road
Haulage Association, was never subject to this legislation, and
in consequence was at all times able to introduce into his conditions of carriage clauses limiting his liability. As a result, the
independent carriers never generally evolved the double tariff
represented by the company's risk and "owner's risk" rates
common in railway goods carriage. Instead, the practice in the
case of these carriers has been to negative their own liability so
far as is possible and to hive off as an insurance operation the
indemnity required by the consignor who is not satisfied with
the very limited responsibility remaining after the standard conditions have made their exclusions. Thus the standard conditions
of the Railways Board, those of the British Road Services and
the new conditions of the Road Haulage Services *tend* to equate
with the traditional common carrier's liability, whilst to obtain
a corresponding contract of carriage with the independent carrier
it is necessary to supplement the standard conditions (which
approximate the "owner's risk" conditions of the Railways) with

[6] By *Peek* v. *N. Staffordshire Railway Co.* (1863) 10 H.L. 473.

an insurance policy. To compare the standard conditions of the Railways Board or of British Road Services with the 1961 standard conditions of the Road Haulage Association members is not therefore to compare like with like.

It is inevitable that in each set of conditions much of the content is concerned with the limitation of liability. Thus in each case there is protection to the carrier in the event of faulty packing or inadequate addressing and against the usual hazards lying outside the carrier's control. When one passes to the question what liability is in fact borne by the carrier the answer is given explicitly in the Railway Conditions and in the British Road Services Conditions thus. In the case of the British Railways Board:

> Subject to these Conditions the Board shall be liable for any loss or misdelivery of or damage to merchandise occasioned during transit as defined by these Conditions unless the Board shall prove that such loss, misdelivery or damage has arisen from:
>
> (a) Act of God.
> (b) Any consequence of war, invasion, act of foreign enemy, hostilities (whether war be declared or not), civil war, rebellion, insurrection, military or usurped power or confiscation, requisition, destruction of or damage to property by or under the order of any government or public or local authority.
> (c) Seizure under legal process.
> (d) Act or omission of the Trader his servants or agents.
> (e) Inherent liability to wastage in bulk or weight, latent defect or inherent defect, vice or natural deterioration of the merchandise.
> (f) Casualty (including fire or explosion).
>
> Provided that:
>
> (i) Where loss, misdelivery or damage arises and the Board have failed to prove that they used all reasonable foresight and care in the carriage of the merchandise the Board shall not be relieved from liability for such loss, misdelivery or damage.
> (ii) The Board shall not incur liability of any kind in

respect of merchandise where there has been fraud on the part of the Trader.

The British Road Services clause is substantially identical:

Subject to these conditions the Carriers shall be liable for any loss or misdelivery of or damage to merchandise occasioned during transit as defined by these conditions unless the Carriers shall prove that such loss, misdelivery or damage has arisen from:

(a) Act of God.

(b) any consequences of war, invasion, act of foreign enemy, hostilities (whether war be declared or not), civil war, rebellion, insurrection, military or usurped power or confiscation, requisition, destruction of or damage to property by or under the order of any government or public or local authority.

(c) seizure under legal process.

(d) Act or omission of the Trader his servants or agents.

(e) inherent liability to wastage in bulk or weight, latent defect or inherent defect, vice or natural deterioration of the merchandise.

(f) insufficient or improper packing.

(g) insufficient or improper labelling or addressing.

(h) riots, civil commotion, strikes, lockouts, stoppage or restraint of labour from whatever cause; or

(j) consignee not taking or accepting delivery within a reasonable time.

Provided that:

(i) where loss, misdelivery or damage arises and the Carriers have failed to prove that they used all reasonable foresight and care in the carriage of the merchandise the Carriers shall not be relieved from liability for such loss, misdelivery or damage.

(ii) The Carriers shall not incur liability of any kind in respect of merchandise where there has been fraud on the part of the Trader.

The 1967 British Road Services clause is almost word for word the same.

It will be noted that the liability is positive and the onus of proof lies upon the carrier to show that damage or loss comes under one or other of the escape clauses. The position under " owner's risk " conditions has long been that the carrier is liable only for loss or damage due to the wilful misconduct of its own servants, but the onus of proof is transferred to the consignor or consignee as the case may be.

The position of the road haulier using the former R.H.A. conditions is worthy of analysis with some care. The conditions which are relevant are:

2. The Contractor is not a common carrier and will accept goods for carriage only on these conditions.

5. The Contractor shall not in any case be liable for:
  (a) Loss of a particular market (whether held daily or at intervals); or
  (b) Indirect or consequential damages; or
  (c) Loss or damage arising from:
    (i) Insufficient or improper packing or addressing; or
    (ii) The perishable, hazardous, fragile or brittle nature or the mechanical derangement of the goods; or
    (iii) Riots, civil commotions, strikes, lockouts, stoppages or restraint of labour from whatever cause, whether partial or general; or
    (iv) Failure by the consignee to take delivery within a reasonable time.

7. In the absence of a special contract between the Contractor and the consignor or consignee the liability of the Contractor in respect of loss or damage to the goods shall in no circumstances exceed the value of the goods and where neither the consignor nor the consignee is the owner thereof then the liability of such consignor or consignee to the owner (whichever is the less) and shall in any case be limited as follows:
  (a) Where the consignment exceeds one quarter of a hundredweight to the sum of £40 per gross hundredweight and *pro rata* for any part of a hundredweight of the goods so lost or damaged; and
  (b) Where the consignment does not exceed one quarter

of a hundredweight to the sum of £10 for the whole
or part of such consignment so lost or damaged.
Provided that the Contractor shall in every event have the
protection of the Carriers Act 1830.

It is clear that there was here no attempt to say in positive
terms what liability was to attach to the carrier. It must be
deduced by noting the exclusions. To begin with, the carrier,
not being a common carrier, was not an insurer of the goods and
was responsible only for the consequences of negligence on the
part of himself, his servants or agents. Clause 5 then proceeded
to exclude indirect damage of various kinds, and certain classes
of damage due to *force majeure*, faulty packing and addressing
(some part of these exclusions being clearly unnecessary since the
carrier, not being a common carrier would not have been liable
in any event). Finally, an overall limit of £10 on small parcels
and £40 per hundredweight was set to liability, and the statutory
protection of the Carriers Act relating to articles of special value
confirmed. Translating this into positive terms, the road carrier
using these conditions of carriage is liable for damage for the
goods themselves up to the limit mentioned provided the damage
is due to the negligence or, of course, wilful misconduct on the
part of his employees. There is therefore a narrow difference
between the " owner's risk " conditions of the railways and the
former Road Haulage Association conditions, a difference resting
in the boundary between " negligence " and " wilful misconduct."
The boundary is not always easy to draw, but is none the less
real. Negligence is the failure to exercise proper care, wilful
misconduct involves the deliberate taking of a wrongful course of
action. The wrongful course of action may include or involve
failure to take care, but for it to be wilful misconduct must go
beyond *mere* carelessness and constitute conscious recklessness.
The boundary may involve consideration of a state of mind; thus
an example [7] :

Suppose a consignment of Cheshire cheese is sent from
Cheshire to London and packed in Cheshire by the railway's
servants who are perfectly familiar with this sort of work.
Suppose further, the servants entrusted with the packing set
aside the method usually applied and pack the cheese in a

[7] Quoted from Kahn-Freund, *op. cit.* p.231.

faulty manner although they know perfectly well that this must lead to a deterioration of the merchandise. This is a case of wilful misconduct, though there is no actual intention to damage the cheese.

If however as in *Lewis* v. *G.W. Ry.*,[8] the cheese is sent from London to Shrewsbury and if an improper mode of packing is applied by servants who are not used to this work, this is, at its worst, negligence. If there is no evidence that the railway servants know that the mode of packing which they adopt is likely to cause injury, they may be blamed for not having made the proper inquiries as to an adequate method of packing. This omission, however, will only be an evidence of carelessness, it does not amount to recklessness.

The extent to which a carrier can confer exemption from liability upon himself by use of extravagantly worded conditions is a moot point. The attempt can be carried very far indeed. Here, for example, is a clause taken from the "Standard Conditions for the Carriage of Goods" of a small shipping company engaged in coastwise trade:

> The Company shall not in any circumstances whatever be liable for any damage, loss, ... detention, deterioration, delay, misdelivery or non-delivery of or to goods ... howsoever, whensoever or wheresoever the same may have been caused even though such damage, loss, deterioration, delay, misdelivery or non-delivery is wholly or partly due to the wrongful act, neglect or default of the Company or its Servants or any other person for whom the Company is or may be responsible and even though any ship or craft in or on which any of the goods may at any time be loaded was unseaworthy at the time of loading or sailing or at any other time. In particular and without limiting the generality of the foregoing provisions, such provisions shall apply whether the goods were on land or water, or in or on any vessel, craft, conveyance or in any other place of any kind, and whether in the custody of the Company or not, and whether during or in the course of collecting, delivery, loading, stowing,

[8] (1877) 3 Q.B.D. 195.

discharging, lighterage, transhipment, storage or otherwise howsoever; . . .

and so on for another 400 or so meaningless words.

Why it should be necessary to use 600 words to say " we accept no liability of any kind in any circumstances " remains a mystery, except that to say it so briefly might permit it to be read, whereas the clause quoted is one of twenty-four clauses, the whole 2,500 words being compressed by the use of villainously small type upon the back of the consignment note, where it is fairly certain that very few consignors will ever read it even if their eyesight permitted. The question how unreasonable conditions may be and still remain effective is one that has been considered from time to time, but thus far the position reached in the courts is unclear. A doctrine is certainly being developed that a party cannot rely upon an exemption clause when the nature of his breach goes to the root of the contract,[9] and the long clause referred to above would certainly be so wide as to purport to excuse many acts and omissions that would be fundamental breaches, as, for example, if the carriers were to receive the goods at their wharf and leave them to rot on the quayside. Another line of argument is that the courts may, on the ground of public policy, refuse to apply a clause which is clearly unreasonable, but this is by no means accepted, although it is known to be the view of at least one of the Law Lords.[10] The rule in *Glynn* v. *Margetson*,[11] already referred to earlier in this book is also very relevant.[12]

Passing from damage to the goods in question of undue delay, the conditions used by British Railways and British Road Services provide:

> The Board shall, subject to these conditions, be liable for loss proved by the Trader to have been caused by delay to, or detention of, or unreasonable deviation in the carriage of merchandise unless the Board prove that such delay or detention or unreasonable deviation has arisen without negligence on the part of the Board, their servants or agents.

[9] *Alexander* v. *Railway Executive* [1951] 2 K.B. 882.
[10] Lord Denning in *John Lee & Son (Grantham)* v. *Railway Executive* [1949] 2 All E.R. 581.
[11] *Glynn* v. *Margetson* [1893] A.C. 351.
[12] See pp. 46–48.

The 1967 Road Haulage Association Conditions take a similar line. The 1961 Road Haulage Association Conditions, however, differ slightly:

> The Contractor shall not be liable for delay or detention of goods or for any loss, damage or deterioration arising therefrom except upon proof that the delay, detention, loss, damage or deterioration was due solely to the wilful negligence of the Contractor or the Contractor's servants.

It will be observed that the onus of proof of loss lies in each case upon the contractor, but in the case of the public undertakings and of undertakings using the 1967 Road Haulage Association Conditions they accept that if loss is proved, the onus of proof rests upon them to prove that there was no negligence on their part if they are to escape liability. Thus if a parcel consigned from London to Birmingham is found a month later lying at Inverness awaiting a claimant, and the owner has suffered loss by its detention, the misdirection will be assumed to be due to negligence by the carriers unless they can prove that it was not, so that the claim is likely to be met. If the parcel has been consigned under the 1961 Road Haulage Association Conditions the onus of proof lies upon the claimant, and he must, to enforce his claim, show "wilful negligence." Since he has no access to the facts of the case, and in all probability no one will have the faintest idea how the parcel arrived where it came to be found, this places him at a considerable disadvantage if the carriers seek to stand upon the letter of the conditions. Further, the concept of "wilful negligence" is a difficult one to understand. "Negligence" is one thing and "wilful misconduct" is another, and each has its place in the definition of the liability of carriers, but "wilful negligence" seems to some degree a contradiction in terms and the term does not appear in the 1967 conditions. It can, almost certainly, never really be proved, although circumstances might lead the court to assume it, since to prove that the negligent action or omission was "wilful" involves entering into the awareness and motives of another.

All of these sets of conditions lay down rules regarding the formulation of claims. All require notification of damage to be made, and claims formulated within the specified times related to the date of consignment or delivery as the case may be.

A good deal of discussion has taken place at various times regarding the effect of a signature being given upon the receipt of goods. It is customary for the carrier to take the position that a signature accompanied by the word " unexamined " is a " clear " signature, whereas it is sometimes assumed by the recipient of goods that the addition of this word gives some protection. There is need for the exercise of commonsense here. It is very clear that the addition of the word " unexamined " does not relieve the trader from the obligation to put forward his claims in time. It is equally clear that if the goods are found damaged upon being unpacked and the claim is lodged within the proper time the fact that an unqualified signature is given simply as an acknowledgment that a package has been received will not prejudice the validity of the claim. It is good practice to qualify a signature with the word " damaged " if there is evidence of any damage on the exterior of the package. The carrier is correct when he regards an " unexamined " signature as a " clear " signature in so far as it is evidence that a package has been delivered with no manifest external signs of damage, but is wrong if and when he tries to convey the impression that it is a clear signature in the sense that he, as carrier, is discharged from any liability that might otherwise attach to him.

One curious consequence is worthy of comment in connection with the two expressions " negligence " and " wilful misconduct." Under standard conditions the Railway is substantially in the position of a common carrier and has a high level of liability. Under " owner's risk " conditions it is liable for " wilful misconduct," which clearly includes pilferage, if it can be proved. The carrier under the 1961 Road Haulage Conditions, not being a common carrier, is liable only for " negligence," to which is appended the gratuitous and inappropriate adjective " wilful." Does a deliberate damage or theft on the part of an employee come within the description of " wilful negligence " ? It would seem not, for in essence negligence is the opposite of a deliberate and contemplated act, and the liability of the carrier would lie more within the rules relating to the responsibility of an employer for the wilful acts of his employees. In a case concerned with the theft of goods by a driver of a road haulage firm's vehicle, the consignor who suffered the loss sought to claim compensation by the argument that the firm had been negligent in employing the driver without taking up references, the man having had a record of crime. This attempt, however, failed. Nor can a criminal act of this kind be represented as being " within the course of employment," so as to involve the employer in vicarious responsibility. The only safeguard for the owner of the goods is to insure.

2. In international trade

Before about 1930 a sharp division existed between the law and practice affecting the carriage of goods within the limits of the United Kingdom and that affecting international carriage. The former was governed by the statutory measures controlling the railways, still unnationalised but operating as statutory companies subject to some governmental oversight, and the practices and increasingly standardised conditions evolved by the road haulage carriers as interpreted by common law. The latter came within the international traditions of seaborne transit, crystallised for the United Kingdom by the Carriage of Goods by Sea Act 1924, which made binding upon United Kingdom traders the system agreed upon in the Hague Rules which were themselves the result of a conference initiated by the International Law Association.

This division still exists, in so far as it is one between home and international transits, but it is less clear because the international trade of the United Kingdom is no longer carried exclusively by sea. An increasing proportion of international freight is carried by air, and the development of vehicle ferries between the United Kingdom and the Continent, coupled with the great increases of permitted weights of road vehicles and the growing orientation of the United Kingdom towards Europe instead of to more distant overseas markets, has given rise to a substantial industry of international road haulage.

International carriage of goods, whether by sea, air or road, differs from carriage within the home territory by a much closer limitation of the freedom of the parties to contract. International conditions of carriage are controlled, the control being, so far as the individual in the United Kingdom is concerned, by statute. But the statutes have in each case followed upon international conferences and have made codes of practice internationally agreed binding by law in the United Kingdom. These statutes are the Carriage of Goods by Sea Act 1924 (embodying the rules evolved as the Hague Rules 1921 and recommended for international adoption by conferences in 1922, 1923 and 1924), the Carriage of Goods by Air Acts 1932, 1961 and 1962 (adopting the recommendations of the Warsaw Convention of 1929 and subsequent revisions) and the Carriage of Goods by Road Act 1965 (adopting the recommendations of the Geneva Convention of 1956).

As a result of these statutes and the fact that broadly similar measures adopting the same rules have been enacted in all the principal commercial countries of the world, the trader is confronted with a uniform code of practice which has international legal sanction and which the carrier has neither the incentive nor the power to vary. In each case the rules of the convention are appended to the Act as a Schedule, and it is to these Schedules that reference should be made. The contract of carriage must necessarily incorporate these Schedules either expressly or by implication.

To go further than this and to make any attempt to analyse the rights and duties of the parties would be impossible here. There are standard books on each subject, and because the contracts are imposed ready made, as it were, they are not properly within the scope of this book. It is, however, proper to give a little attention to the use of the shorthand expressions like f.o.b., c.i.f. and the rest, which are sometimes collectively described as " the contracts of commerce."

Every international contract for the sale and purchase of goods is likely to introduce one of these expressions, generally as a qualification of the price of the goods. Thus the sale of a commodity at a price of £x f.o.b. (free on board) means that for the price quoted the seller will provide the goods, pay for carriage to the port of shipment, and all dock dues up to the point when the goods are lifted from the quay and placed on the ship, from which point the buyer begins to be responsible for all costs of transit. The other familiar expression c.i.f. (cost insurance freight) means that in addition the buyer will bear the cost of insurance and freight.

In addition to the familiar f.o.b. and c.i.f. the more important expressions used are

c.and f.: cost and freight (buyer responsible for insurance)

f.a.s.: free alongside ship
f.o.r.: free on rail
ex works: buyer takes all responsibility from the seller's works.

There are in all something more than twenty internationally recognised expressions of this kind, and although their general import is understood uniformly everywhere, the law and practice of different countries and even the practice in different ports can manifest marginal deviations. In order to encourage complete precision the International Chamber of Commerce has issued two authoritative documents. One is called *Incoterms* with a more complete sub-title *International Rules for the Interpretation of Trade Terms*, and contains a precise definition indicating what in the Chamber's view is the division of the incidental costs of carriage between each party. If the parties to a contract agree that the definition of Incoterms is to apply, no argument is possible. The other publication is *Trade Terms 1953* which sets out in detail the actual marginal differences of interpretation as between some twenty of the countries of the world.

PART 2

OTHER COMMERCIAL CONTRACTS

NOTE

In the remaining chapters of this book, the method of treatment will differ considerably from that used in Chapters 2–5. These chapters dealt with a group of typical contractual relationships which tend to be established on the basis of common form sets of clauses which are put forward by one side or the other in the expectation or the hope that they will be accepted as they stand, and which, because of the frequency of the transactions concerned or the authority with which the conditions are endowed by reason of their professional sponsors, do tend to be accepted without demur and without critical examination. In the typical contractual situations which will be examined in the remaining chapters there is not the same tendency. It is true that in some of those situations undertakings may have a printed form which they customarily use, such as a standard form of agency agreement, or contract of employment. They tend, however, to be critically examined in such cases by the other side, principally because the form used is not common to a trade or industry as a whole but is printed primarily for the convenience of one party only and because, unlike the sale or purchase of goods, the contract, though one of a series to one party is not so to the other. Thus an undertaking may use a standard form for a contract of apprenticeship or for granting a licence under a patent of wide application, but to the apprentice or to the licensee the agreement comes as an important incident and is read carefully by him.

The chapters that follow will not therefore be based upon given standard forms, but will aim at discussing some of the practical considerations which must be borne in mind in the framing and negotiation of the agreements in question. It is hoped that this method of treatment may be found useful.

Chapter 6

INSURANCE

INSURANCE is a large and specialised subject. From its tentative beginnings in the sixteenth century and even earlier it has grown to become an immense world-wide industry, with its own professional experts and a considerable library of technical literature. Within the compass of this chapter, necessarily brief, it is neither possible nor desirable to embark upon any general statement of insurance law, but rather to concentrate upon certain features of the insurance contract which call for care in its negotiation and use in practical business life.

The whole field of insurance is traditionally divided into four areas, known in the insurance profession as life, fire, accident and marine. By some quirk of history one speaks of life *assurance*, fire and accident *insurance*, but there is apparently no legal difference between the meaning of the two terms. It is sometimes argued that the word " assurance " is proper in relation to a risk that is bound to eventuate some time, though it may not be possible to forecast when, as in the case of death, so that it is proper to apply the word to life policies. On this argument the proper use of " insurance " is in respect of hazards that are mere possibilities, such as fire and accident. The semantic argument breaks down in the customary use of "the assured" in marine risks.

Each of these principal subjects has gathered round itself a number of associated risks, so that the " life " department of an insurance company also deals with pension schemes, the " fire " department with policies covering the insured against the associated risks of storm, tempest and the like. " Accident " may include all kinds of miscellaneous risks, and marine policies, while primarily concerned with ships and cargoes, may also for traditional reasons, be applied to almost anything. However, although this division is traditional, it is not always followed, and some new types of insurance are treated as major divisions on their own account.

The classical definition of an insurance contract is that contained in a judgment more than 160 years old.[1] It is a contract

---

[1] *Lucena* v. *Crawford* (1808) 127 E.R. 858 (H.L.).

by which " one party, in consideration of a price paid to him adequate to the risk, becomes security to the other that he shall not suffer loss damage or prejudice by the happening of the perils specified to certain things which may be exposed to them." In this definition the words " adequate to the risk " are inexact. All that is necessary is that the price, *i.e.* the premium, should be agreed. In entering into insurance as a business contract it is necessary in the light of this definition to have complete precision as to (a) what is insured, and (b) against what perils it is insured. It is also necessary to recognise that a contract of insurance is basically one of indemnity. Its function is to make good a loss or injury, and if the happening of the event insured against does not involve the insured in any loss there is on the face of things no right to receive payment of any claim, even though a premium has been paid. This generalisation, however, cannot be expressed as a rigid rule. It does not, for example, apply when an insurance policy expressly provides for reinstatement of damage to be " as new." Nor does it apply in the case of life assurance except in those instances in which the insured's interest in the life assured is solely financial as the interest of a creditor in the life of his debtor or of an employer in the life of an employee. In these last two instances the rule is applied not so as to deny liability on the part of the insurer, but to require any balance of insurance money over the true interest of the insurer to be held in trust for the estate of the deceased.

Insurance is one of those activities which has an impact upon private life as well as upon industrial and commercial life. Everyone is acquainted with the normal procedures of obtaining insurance cover by completing a proposal form and having a policy issued. From the point of view of this study what is intended is to subject this commonplace operation to the kind of scrutiny which must be applied to the other contracts of business and by seeking precision to draw attention to some of the special points which, in a business background, must be understood and watched.

It cannot be too strongly emphasised that insurance is a large field and one sometimes calling for expert knowledge. Because this is so there has grown up the profession of " insurance broker," a specialist whose precise niche in the business structure should be understood. Most large businesses and many small ones use the services of insurance brokers in placing their business, and some of the largest of all have insurance departments within their own organisations which operate as though they were brokers. The broker is not an agent. An "insurance agent" sells insurance as the representative of the insurance company, being remunerated by a commission. The broker, just as the agent, is remunerated by commission, but instead of representing the insurance company, he is a professional practitioner working in the interest of his client, the insured. The employment of an insurance broker to take charge of the whole of one's insurances ensures expert oversight,[2] and is a desirable practice. However, just as the possession of a firm of solicitors as one's legal advisers does not render an understanding of one's commercial contracts unnecessary, it is eminently desirable to see the insurance contract for what it is.

1. The proposal and the policy

The completion of a proposal form is usual but not invariable as the first step in effecting insurance. It is not the practice in marine insurance, and in the larger fire risks it is frequently by-passed. In a business possessing a number of properties it is the practice to have a single policy covering all of them, with a schedule listing what is covered, the schedule being amended by additions and deletions as properties are acquired or disposed of. In such cases an annual review with an inspection of the properties is the usual practice.

Where a proposal form is used, it operates as an offer, and the acceptance of the offer brings the contract into existence. It is at the stage of completion of the proposal form that two important features of the law as it affects the insurance contract must be noted. The first is that the contract of insurance is one of those governed by the principle enshrined in the Latin phrase *uberrima fides,* "the utmost good faith," and the other is the special meaning of the word "warranty" in insurance.

The principle of the utmost good faith as applied to insurance is that it is incumbent upon the insured not only to have been

---

[2] Or should do. One should be satisfied that a broker is really an expert, for there is no compulsory qualification called for before a person can so describe himself.

truthful in his actual statements, but to have disclosed to the insurer anything which he knows, or ought to know, might reasonably influence the insurer in accepting or rejecting the risk, whether or not the specific information is asked for. In practice the proposal form will invariably include a question which will focus attention to this consideration. The concealment of any fact which the proposer knows to be material amounts to fraud and may vitiate the contract. If therefore circumstances are known to the proposer which make the risk insured against greater than would otherwise appear, the facts should be made clear.

It will generally be found that a proposal form ends with a " declaration " which not only underlines this aspect of the proposal as involving the utmost good faith, but also states that the proposer " warrants " that the answers given are true and complete and that the proposal is to be incorporated into and to form the basis of the contract. The words " warrant " and " warranty " have a special meaning in insurance, based in part upon a definition in the Marine Insurance Act 1906, and in part upon usage in the insurance business. In the ordinary law of contract a " warranty " is defined as a promise collateral to the contract, breach of which may entitle the aggrieved party to damages but not to rescind the contract.[3] In insurance law a warranty must be strictly and literally complied with; any breach gives the right to the insurer to repudiate the contract and, in effect, to reject a claim. Thus any inaccuracy in the statements made in the proposal or any omission of material information can have the effect of justifying the insurer, at a later date, in rejecting a claim under the policy.

The issue of a policy normally follows the acceptance of the proposal, but if acceptance of the proposal is intimated in any other way, for example, by letter indicating that cover has been given and that the policy will be issued in due course, it is this acceptance of the offer contained in the proposal which brings the contract into existence, and, so far as the existence of a binding contract is concerned, it is immaterial whether the policy is issued or not. But the purpose of the policy is, of course, to provide a proper document embodying all the terms of the contract. The standard form of policy should be examined and

---

[3] Although the Misrepresentation Act 1967 has modified this in the contract of sale.

read at the time the proposal is made, because the proposal form is an offer to enter into a contract in the terms of the standard policy and if this contains conditions and exclusions as a result of which cover is not so extensive as was expected it is no answer to say that this was not known at the time the proposal was made.   Even so, the proposal form will have stated that the proposal is to be incorporated into and to form the basis of the contract, and the policy, in its turn, will recite that the proposal has been made and that it, with its declaration, is to be the basis of the contract and deemed to be incorporated therein, so in any insurance contract the proposal and the policy must be taken together as constituting the contract document.   The general rule of interpretation by which, once a contract is reduced to a single comprehensive document, other extraneous documents are deemed to be thereby excluded, does not apply so as to constitute the policy a contract document to the exclusion of the proposal.

2. Law and practice

One of the difficulties attending the precise definition of one's rights and duties under a contract of insurance arises from the fact that all reputable British insurers tend to interpret their obligations liberally rather than in any legalistic manner.   They regard their operations as a service to their policy holders rather than as a series of contractual situations at which they should look narrowly to interpret each to their own best advantage.   To give a simple example, the normal provision written into the " conditions " of a motor insurance policy is that the " policy holder shall . . . maintain in an efficient condition " any car insured.   There is no definition of " efficient," and the word is not even qualified by " reasonably."   If when an accident happens it is found that brakes, steering or anything else was defective, this condition must presumably have been broken, but it is only in the most blatant cases of this kind that the better companies disown liability.   Thus in *Jones and James* v. *Provincial* [4] the condition was held to have been breached when the insured had driven without a footbrake, which he had himself removed. But just how neglectful one may be of the condition of one's car without breaking the conditions has never been tested in the

[4] (1929) 46 T.L.R. 71.

courts with precision, and the same applies with other types of insurance.

This, however, leads to a commonsense reflection affecting insurance policies and their scrutiny. It is that quite clearly an insurer will be far more likely to stand on his legal rights when a claim is large than when it is small. Therefore, in considering the importance of examining the policy to ensure that they are being observed special diligence should be observed in those policies which are of a nature to involve the possibility of very large claims. This applies particularly to fire, third party, and employers' liability insurance.

3. Insurable interest

For an insurance policy to be valid in law, it is necessary for the insured to have an insurable interest, which means that if the event happened against which he is insured, he would, apart from his insurance, suffer loss. This principle has sometimes been very strictly applied, and where there is a situation of associated companies it is important to ensure that the company which is insured is the same as that which suffers loss in the event of the hazard becoming a reality. In one case frequently quoted [5] the insured had a fire policy on timber which he had cut and sold to a company of which he was the sole shareholder. The timber was destroyed by fire. It was held that because the ownership had passed to the company, a separate person in law, he had no insurable interest and could therefore support no claim; the fact that the company was his own and merely a means of handling his business did not prevail. There is a simple way of overcoming this possibility where because of companies being interlocked it may be possible for ownership to be transferred frequently from one to another. This is for all policies to be on a group basis in which all the companies are included "for their respective rights and interests." This is particularly important where the companies within a group are concerned with different stages in a production process, or with the manufacture or purchase of components ultimately assembled in an associated company's works. In such a situation there may be frequent invoicing from one company to another within a single management

[5] *Macaura* v. *Northern Assurance Company* [1925] A.C. 619.

structure, so that property rights often change in the stock in trade and work in progress.

4. Liability insurance

Although there are standard liability policies which are offered to the general public, liability insurance belongs for the main part to the business world, and deserves some comment. It includes three main types of risk. In the " public liability " sector is the risk of some member of the public suing an undertaking for damage suffered or alleged to be suffered because of some accident in the course of its operations, or for the state of its buildings. " Employers' liability " covers the responsibility of this undertaking to its own employees in respect of accidents at work due to some negligence.[5a] " Product liability " is concerned with the risk of persons claiming as a result of faults in ones products indicating negligence in their manufacture. These are all areas in which it is necessary for the skill of the insurance expert, probably a broker, to be called upon but to be assisted by one's own specialised knowledge of one's own business, and in each instance it is of great importance to read the policies carefully to ensure that the conditions are being observed. One requirement which recurs in the conditions attaching to such policies is the notification to the insurers of changes occurring in the nature of the business, or, in the case of employers' liability, in the occupations followed or the undertaking of work involving special risks. Another is the requirement that the entire conduct of any negotiation of any claim should be left to the insurers. This can, in some circumstances, operate so as to appear contrary to one's interests, as when one would prefer to settle a claim quietly without publicity rather than fight it thus avoiding adverse publicity. It is necessary to count the cost in this regard. There are circumstances in which the interests of the insurer and insured are contrary.

Insurances of this kind are customarily handled on a declaration basis. This means that at the outset an estimate of the basis on which the premium is calculated, whether wages, turnover, or some other criterion, is made and the initial premium paid thereon. At regular intervals a declaration is made of the actual

[5a] From January 1972 a legal obligation rests on most employers to carry Employers' Liability insurance (Employers' Liability (Compulsory Insurance) Act 1969).

figures in arrear, and a continuous correction of premiums introduced.

It is always unwise to seek to economise on insurance premiums in these types of insurance by failing to pitch the maximum indemnity at a sufficient magnitude. Premiums do not rise *pro rata*. It costs little more to have a maximum of £1,000,000 than of £100,000, and as a matter of business policy it is the really large claim that can spell ruin and against which therefore one needs protection by way of insurance.[5b]

What has already been said about the practice of insurers in construing their obligations liberally rather than legally applies in this type of cover. The conditions will almost inevitably require the insured to observe proper standards of operation, safe methods of working, compliance with Factories Act requirements and the like. Many accidents occur because, due to human frailty, there has been laxity in doing these very things. Because so much depends upon the relationship with the insurer and the standard which the insurer deserves and the reputation he has gained, what is called for in the conduct of this business as with all types of insurance is a full and honest disclosure of the facts at all stages whether of proposal or claim, and a close liaison with a competent expert.

5. Marine insurance

Marine insurance by which is primarily meant the insurance of ships and, more important, the insurance of goods in transit by sea, differs from other branches of insurance in a number of ways. This is because of its antiquity, its international character and its history. It was known as long ago as the thirteenth century as a practice of the Lombards, those pioneers of international trade, and in England was developed through the formative period by the unique institution of " Lloyd's " in the City of London, named after Lloyd's Coffee House, which, appropriately enough, was located in Lombard Street in the City of London.[6] Because of the need for the precise terms of insurance cover to be standardised for international use, it has become

---

[5b] In the case of Employers' Liability a maximum of £2 m. in respect of any one occurrence is made mandatory by regulation.

[6] Its earliest location was in Tower Street. For a brief history of Lloyd's and its special association with Marine Insurance see article " Lloyd's " in the *Encyclopaedia Britannica*.

the subject of legislation to a greater extent than any other branches of insurance. Whereas in other branches of insurance a policy is not legally necessary (though usual) and its form and content a matter for the insurer's draftsman or for agreement between the parties, a contract of marine insurance cannot be enforced in the absence of a formal policy, and the form of policy is laid down by statute in Schedule 1 of the Marine Insurance Act 1906. The whole subject is a large and specialised one in relation to which the student should consult works of a specialist nature.[7]

A number of specialised procedures are followed, and the insurance of goods shipped, whether by the exporter or the importer according to the terms of sale, is in practice handled by the shippers who " declare " the shipment as coming within the scope of the appropriate policy. The machinery most frequently used is that the exporter or importer maintains with the insurer a single policy which may cover all his shipments for a given period or up to a specified sum, or to or from a specific country, and " declares " each shipment as it is made, with particulars of the nature and value of the merchandise and the name of the ship.

The practice of marine insurance broking is to a large degree integrated with that of shipping agency. Thus an exporting organisation will engage a firm of shipping agents who will co-ordinate all the operations necessary from the time the goods leave the exporter's factory until they are placed on board the carrying vessel. The shipping agents will have all the necessary information regarding the exporter's " open," " floating " or " blanket " cover, which indeed they themselves may have organised. Within the scope of those policies they will issue or secure the issue of insurance certificates which, though not legally policies, are customarily accepted as evidence of insurance and form part of the shipping documents relating to the consignment.

6. Export credit guarantees

Another highly specialised branch of insurance is that by which an exporter who has sent goods away without having

[7] A useful summary is contained in Chap. 23 of *The Export Trade* by Schmit-thoff (5th ed. 1969).

received payment is compensated if the buyer of those goods fails to pay. Because the danger of default is governed largely by political considerations, as when foreign exchange difficulties result in a whole country defaulting, the commercial insurance market is not willing to underwrite this risk, and the Export Credit Guarantee Department, operating under the Department of Trade and Industry (the former Board of Trade) has a virtual monopoly in the field. In this class of business, the insurance contract is between the Department and the exporter, and its existence (at least, in theory) is not known to the overseas customer. The policy, which must be one of a limited number of standard types issued by the Department tailored to different classes of export business, is normally issued annually and declarations, made in arrear, are the basis of premium payment. Naturally, to obtain the protection afforded by these policies, the exporter must surrender some of his freedom to negotiate terms of payment with his customer, especially when long credit is sought.

CHAPTER 7

THE CONTRACT OF EMPLOYMENT

NEXT to the contract for the sale of goods, the contract of employment is probably the most ubiquitous in business life. It involves every concern which has grown beyond the state of the one-man business or simple partnership, and from the point of view of the employee, it governs the livelihood of about half of the population in any developed country. It is interesting to notice how its history has affected our mental attitude to the employer/employee relationship. In pure legal theory the contract of employment like most other contracts, is a consensual one in which the parties are free agents until they agree as equals to enter into the contract that binds them both. Employment, however, is rooted in slavery, and is, indeed, the classic example of the way in which over the course of millennia the course of social changes has been from status to contract, according to the broad theoretical generalisation of that great jurist Sir Henry Maine.[1] Through various changes and under different social and economic pressures the ancient institution of slavery broke down, as did the serfdom of the feudal system in our own country. However, the personal attachment of the servant to the master through the period of change continued to fall far short of the theoretical freedom of contract beloved by legal and economic theorists of the nineteenth century. Long after the feudal relationship had broken down and the last incidents of feudalism had been abolished, the hierarchical relationship of master and servant persisted, as is illustrated by the fact that personal violence committed by a servant against his master was deemed " petty treason " and visited with a more serious sanction than the same act between equals. Similarly, the young employee was most commonly an apprentice over whom his master held powers of discipline, restraint, and punishment quite inconsistent with any concept of their relationship being one between equals. The master assumed without question

[1] Maine, *Ancient Law*.

the right to chastise his personal servant.   So Antonio of Syracuse declares:

> " Now, as I am a Christian, answer me
> In what safe place you have bestowed my money;
> Or shall I break that merry sconce of yours . . .
> Where is the thousand marks thou hadst of me? "

To which Dromio of Ephesus replies:

> " I have some marks of yours upon my pate
> Some of my mistress' marks upon my shoulders,
> But not a thousand marks between you both. . . . " [2]

It may perhaps still be discerned as a lingering relic of the concept of " status " that we are still expected to describe ourselves on many printed forms, and are still described in legal documents, by our occupations, and this even when the occupation is completely irrelevant to the purpose of the document, whilst the practices of the craft trade unions, which have always been entrenched citadels of conservatism in anything but the political sense of the word, have made it so nearly impossible for a man to move from one craft to another that, in the social environments where they are dominant, " status " is being sustained as a very real fact.

Out of the mental atmosphere of this kind of relationship the modern contract of employment has emerged.   The change has, however, been due less to the law than to the slow movement of social growth and the modification of institutions, and especially to the decreasing influence of the individual employer by comparison with the large corporate organisation.   Today, although there are still very many personal employers, the vast majority of employees work for public bodies or limited companies.   Thus it can be safely said that the typical contract of employment today is between an individual employee and a corporate employer. As has been said, however, the change in concept is one that has arisen from the change in the shape of society: little has been done by legislation to alter the outward concept of the employment relationship until the recent enactment of the Contracts of Employment Act 1963.

[2] *Comedy of Errors*, Act I, Scene 2.

Although this measure was not a far-reaching one, its requirement that certain terms of every contract of employment be reduced to writing threw a new emphasis upon those details which in the employer/employee relationship have in the recent past frequently been left to custom. Thus far, most of the law of master and servant has been case law. It has tended to lag behind social changes [3] and the amelioration of the lot of the employee is owed principally to the combined effect of the power of trade unions, a sense of social conscience and the increasing wealth of society as a whole due to technological advance. Which of the three factors has been the most important can be a matter of opinion.

Looking at the normal pattern of employment immediately prior to the coming into force of the Contracts of Employment Act 1963, the following is probably a fair summary of the situation:

(a) The large majority of contracts of employment were not evidenced in writing as between employer and employee, but in many cases some part of the obligations of both parties were regulated by overall contracts entered into between trade unions and federations of employers or large corporate employers. These are sometimes developed in great detail through the adoption of " working rules " often worked out at a district level.

(b) In most appointments of a clerical, administrative, or technical nature the contract of employment was initiated by some letter of appointment, but many of the detailed terms were left unwritten, and subsequent changes, such as increases of salary or altered privileges, were seldom put into writing.

(c) The full " service agreement " was entered into for the most part with the senior executive whose appointment was for a period of years.

(d) A number of large employers used a printed form of agreement for the purpose of defining the special conditions relating to the apprentice.

The requirement of the Contracts of Employment Act 1963 is

---

[3] Consider, for example, the melancholy history of the doctrine of common employment, established in *Priestley* v. *Fowler* (1837) 3 M. & W. 1 and only abolished finally by the Law Reform (Personal Injuries) Act 1948.

not that the contract of employment shall be in writing, but that within three months from the commencement of employment (provided the employment lasts so long) there must be furnished to the employee a " statement in writing " setting out the terms of the contract of employment in respect of certain specified matters. The effect of the Act is therefore bound to be that much which in categories (a) and (b) above has in the past left implicit will in the future become explicit, and it is likely to have the effect that the practice of providing a full written contract of service will tend to apply to a larger class than it has heretofore.

The precise requirement of the Act in this regard was as follows:

> " Not later than thirteen weeks after the beginning of an employee's period of employment with an employer, the employer shall give to the employee a written statement identifying the parties, specifying the date when the employment began, and giving the following particulars of the terms of the employment as at a specified date not more than one week before the statement is given, that is—
>
> (a) the scale or rate of remuneration, or the method of calculating the remuneration,
>
> (b) the intervals at which remuneration is paid (that is, weekly or monthly, or by some other period),
>
> (c) any terms and conditions relating to hours of work (including any terms and conditions relating to normal working hours),
>
> (d) any terms and conditions relating to—
>> (i) holidays and holiday pay,
>> (ii) incapacity for work due to sickness or injury, including any provisions for sick pay,
>> (iii) pension and pension schemes, and
>
> (e) the length of notice which the employee is obliged to give and entitled to receive to determine his contract of employment:
>
> Provided that paragraph (d) (iii) of this subsection shall not apply to the employees of any body or authority if the employees' pension rights depend on the terms of a pension scheme established under any provision contained in or having effect under an Act of Parliament and the body or

authority are required by any such provision to give to new employees information concerning their pension rights, or concerning the determination of questions affecting their pension rights." [4]

A further nine subsections elaborate this requirement and answer some of the questions which will arise in practice. Subsection (4) provides that if any change takes place in the particulars which have to be included in the statement, a written statement of the change is to be delivered to the employee within one month. Thus in any organisation where increases of salary were formerly notified to the employee only by word of mouth it is now necessary, in order to comply with the law, for a written confirmation to follow.

It is, however, provided in subsection (5) that it will be permissible as an alternative for any of the particulars required by subsection (1) or any amendment required by subsection (4) to be contained in a written statement to be contained in " some document which the employee has reasonable opportunities of reading in the course of his employment, or which is made reasonably accessible to him in some other way." It is the custom in some undertakings for much of the required information to be contained in a book of staff regulations, or, where there is an active union representative, for the conditions of employment to be included in a national agreement or set of working rules. This will render unnecessary much that otherwise would call for inclusion in the written statement.

Some of the details called for by the Act required elaboration, and to some degree the Industrial Relations Act 1971 supplied this, requiring specifically that the terms and conditions relating to holidays were to be set out in sufficient detail to enable the employee's entitlement, including any entitlement to accrued holiday pay on termination of employment, to be precisely calculated. It also added a requirement that the " statement " should specify a person to whom and a procedure by which any grievance on the part of the employee in connection with the employment should be reported and negotiated on. Even so, much is still lacking in precision.

For example, it is uncertain how much detail is necessary

[4] Contracts of Employment Act 1963, s. 4 (1).

in connection with pension schemes, rights of the employer and employee in the matter of the dating of holidays as distinct from their duration, or the right of the employer to make changes in actual working hours. It is clear that the " scale or rate of remuneration or the method of calculating remuneration " must include reference to overtime rates or piece-work calculation if these apply. It is a matter of practical application of the Act that the methods of calculating some group bonus systems are extremely complicated and will be difficult to embody in the " statement in writing."

The need to specify in writing the rights of the employee in the matter of sick pay may constitute a problem in many small or medium businesses where, although categories of employees who possess what is generally regarded as " staff " status have had the right to be paid during periods of sickness medically certified, the maximum period for such payment has never been laid down, each case being dealt with on its merits. It would seem that in such cases there would be no reason why a minimum period should not be specified, with the rider that the management would in suitable cases continue to make payment on an *ex gratia* basis without commitment.[5] If it is the practice to deduct from sick pay the amount of benefit receivable from National Insurance this fact should be mentioned.

The fact that these statements are required by the million has ensured that the legal publishers have studied the requirements and produced common form drafts for completion by the addition of names and other details, and for this reason no further comment is necessary here.

Attention may, however, be directed to the full contract of service, which is commonly entered into in respect of senior employees. As has been pointed out, the " Statement " under the Act is not a contract: it is a summary of the provisions of a contract already existing. That the need to supply it will not arise if the contract itself is in writing and deals with all the points mentioned in section 4 (1) is likely to encourage large employers to use full written contracts for wider categories of employee. What may be called a full service agreement is already commonly used for:

---

[5] The wording used should be framed in recognition of the fact that to say that a payment is *ex gratia* is not in itself conclusive that no legal right exists (*Edwards* v. *Skyways Ltd.* [1964] 1 W.L.R. 349).

(a) higher executives or employees of professional or technological status,

(b) directors who, in addition to their directorships, have executive or departmental duties,

(c) employees proceeding overseas for tours of duty.

The higher executive, professional employee or technologist, especially if newly engaged from outside the employing company's organisation, is likely to be in a position to negotiate, and the service agreement is entered into between equals in a sense that the contract of employment in humbler ranks is not. The principal content of such a negotiated agreement will differ from the ordinary contract of employment and will include special provisions.

(a) It will be expressed to be for a term, probably for some years, this being in the interest of both parties, during which time the employee is to devote his whole time and attention to the employer's business in the capacity to which he is being appointed. This obviously has to be interpreted with reason, and it is generally added that during the period of the agreement he is not to be engaged in any other gainful occupation but that no restriction is placed on his freedom to be interested as a shareholder or debenture holder in other businesses.

(b) It is not uncommon for the remuneration of the higher executive, especially if his duties are such as directly to influence the profits of the organisation, to be related to profits or to turnover. Where this is the case, a close definition of profits may be necessary and it is usual, in the case of a company, for the auditors to be made the arbiters of any dispute or difference of opinion.

(c) Provisions will be included in respect of the entitlement of the employee to reimbursement of expenses or to any fixed allowance for expenses. This may include, *inter alia,* the provision of a car, in which the mileage or other allowance in connection therewith will be defined.

(d) The pension arrangements, instead of being limited to

membership of a company pension scheme, may involve special payments to an insurance policy made direct by the employing company, which may seek to obtain tax and/or estate duty benefit for the employee by retaining some nominal discretion as to the ultimate disposal of the policy.

(e) It is usual for the employer to reserve the right to terminate the agreement in the event of a complete breakdown in health on the part of the employee, but apart from this provision the remuneration is likely to be payable for longer periods of incapacity than is usual in the case of other employees.

(f) One important and potentially disputable matter is the degree of restraint if any to be placed upon the employee at the end of the term of employment, from entering the service of a competitor or engaging in any other pursuit where his knowledge could be used to damage the former employer. This is subject to the general provisions of the law regarding contracts in restraint of trade. It will be recollected that the general rule is that a contract in restraint of trade is contrary to the public interest and is for this reason not enforceable, but that the law makes an exception in enforcing such contracts where the restraint is reasonable. What is reasonable is a question of fact, and the question to be asked is whether the restraint proposed goes farther than is necessary to protect the legitimate interest of the promisee, in this case, the employer. It is important, in framing this type of clause, to remember that if the clause is unreasonable, it will be unenforceable. If, therefore, it is desired that such a clause be inserted in a service agreement, the interest of the employing company will be best served by taking care that it is clearly not in any way vindictive and is designed to do no more than to prevent the employee from using inside knowledge of the business to the detriment of the employer, whilst not preventing him from pursuing his calling in some permitted sphere.

(g) It is usual to provide that the employing company may terminate the contract of employment summarily in the event of the employee becoming insolvent or being convicted of any crime. Since, however, " crime " covers anything from a parking offence to high treason, it is usual to qualify this by invoking this sanction only if the crime is serious. The former definition often used, " indictable " is now obsolete, and " arrestable " is more suitable. It is sometimes the practice to include the right for the employee to be summarily dismissed if he is guilty of any " misconduct " in connection with the business, the words sometimes being added " of which the directors shall be the sole judges." It can only be said that for the employing company such a clause would be dangerous ground on which to fight an action, since it is clearly repugnant to the rule of natural justice – *nemo judex in causa sua* – a man should not be judge in his own cause.

(h) In the case of appointments of a scientific or technological nature, it is usual to provide that if the employee makes any invention in the course of his term of employment he must disclose this and permit the employer to apply for patent protection in its own name. The agreement should also clarify the rights of the employee in any such invention if the employer does not wish to avail itself either of the invention or its right to patent.

(j) If an appointment is for a defined period and is not envisaged as continuing beyond that period, a clause may be included declaring that on its termination no payment under the Redundancy Payments Act 1965 is to be due.

An interesting practical question is how valuable a service agreement is to the employer and to the employee. In the case of an employee with special abilities, knowledge, or connections there is little doubt that in a period of business expansion he is liable to lose more than he gains by entering into a term of agreement, since he forfeits his liberty to move. The employing company forfeits much less, for if it ejects the employee in breach of the contract the only sanction the law will enforce is the payment of damages, the quantum of which is fairly readily assessable.   Thus the employing company which is dissatisfied with its bargain can buy its release at a known price, whereas the dissatisfied employee is less likely to take the law into his own hands for fear that his present employer might attempt to proceed by injunction against the prospective employer to whom he wishes to transfer before the end of the term.   Although such an action would be a very doubtful venture, the possibility causes it to have a nuisance value and deters an employer from seeking to persuade a potential employee from repudiating or seeking escape from an existing agreement.

When a senior executive is also a director, or is to be appointed as a director, it is important to recognise that the service agreement dealing with the executive appointment may be in conflict with the articles of association, which regulate the appointment and resignation or removal of directors, especially if and when either the company or the employee director wishes to terminate the appointment otherwise than as provided in the agreement.   If the executive appointment is necessarily based upon the director-ship and is dependent upon the continuation of the directorship, it should not be overlooked that the agreement will not override the articles of association, and although it is usual for articles to provide that directors holding executive appointments are not to be subject to retirement by rotation, they normally provide that one of the regular ways in which any directorship ends is by resignation.   Indeed, it can be argued that a director cannot be divested nor even divest himself of the right to resign, since resignation is his only effective way of disassociating himself from liability in the event of the board as a whole pursuing a course which he regards as involving personal liabilities which he is not prepared to accept.[6]   When the company is a subsidiary, or is in the control of an individual personal shareholder, there is also the possibility, on the other side, of the exercise by the controlling shareholders of the statutory powers created by section 184 of the Companies Act, under which the office of any director can be

---

[6] If, for example, a proposed course is *ultra vires* and would involve him in personal liability.

terminated by the adverse vote of the shareholders at a general meeting provided special notice is given.

It may be argued, although the point is not free from doubt, that by accepting a term appointment as an executive, in a capacity dependent upon his continuing as a director, the appointee has by implication undertaken not to use the device of resignation from the directorship as a means of prematurely terminating the executive appointment. Since, however, it is always safer to rely upon express than implied terms, the proper course is to insert in the agreement an undertaking on the part of the employee that he will not resign from his directorship during the term of the appointment. It may, however, be questioned whether even an express term would remove from him the absolute right to resign on a point of conscience, and it is quite certain that if he were to resign in due manner as provided in the articles of association the resignation would be effective, and the only remedy of the employing company would lie in damages. For the protection of the employee against action under section 184 of the Companies Act 1948 nothing would be of any effect short of joining the controlling shareholder as a party to the agreement, undertaking that the power to terminate the directorship would not be exercised, but it would be proper to insert a provision for the payment of compensation should the appointment be terminated in this way, since in the last resort the power of the shareholders to remove a director cannot be overridden, and the ownership of shares can change.

Passing to the third category of employee customarily made the subject of a full service agreement, the employee who is undertaking a tour of duty overseas, a number of special considerations apply. Among the most important are these:

    (a) In addition to remuneration, it is frequently necessary to provide the employee with accommodation and also to provide for medical costs to be met by the employing company. The extent to which the cost of removal of personal effects is to be met by the employing company should be specified. Further, it is desirable to write into an agreement some provision for the adjustment of the remuneration in the event of serious changes in the cost of living in the overseas country, or the discovery of significant factors unknown when the agreement was negotiated.

(b) The costs of travelling to the appointment and return at the end of the tour of duty must be provided for, including the question of repatriation in the event of the appointment being terminated prematurely, either on account of sickness or unsuitability or through circumstances unforeseen at the time the contract was entered into.

(c) In the case of tours of duty in tropical countries it is usual for the United Kingdom employee to be granted, in addition to local leave in accordance with practice in the territory, a period of several months home leave at the end of a period of several years, frequently three years. Facilities are usually available through associations of employers for practice in this regard to be compared and assimilated, and this is to be commended, because the United Kingdom employees in distant territories have a great deal of social contact and compare their relative privileges.

(d) When remuneration is expressed to be paid in a foreign currency where the employee is to be resident, it is wise to introduce a clause providing for changes in the relative value of currencies. If the agreement provides for the employee to claim adjustment of remuneration in the event of any substantial change occurring in the cost of living it is advisable to provide for arbitration in the event of failure to reach agreement. Arbitration can well be placed with a firm of accountants possessing offices in both the home and overseas territory.

(e) If pension rights are involved, care should be taken to ensure that the practice regarding deduction of contributions and the intention regarding benefit is not in conflict with the law of the territory. In the case of appointments which are clearly unlikely to be permanent it is sometimes necessary to keep the pension arrangements alive in the United Kingdom, since the uncertainties of the present time and the impossibility of foreseeing the economic possibilities in a distant future render it desirable to avoid building up pension rights for an employee in a territory other than his home country, since he might have to remain an exile in order to enjoy them.

CHAPTER 8

PATENT LICENCES AND " KNOW-HOW " AGREEMENTS

THE agreements to be discussed in this chapter constitute a class of special importance in manufacturing industry. When their subject-matter is closely analysed the patent licence and the agreement for the sale of " know-how " represent situations which, from the point of view of the law, are fundamentally dissimilar, and which, furthermore, present quite different problems for the draftsman. For reasons of practical technical common sense, however, they cannot always be disentangled because the situation which calls for the one frequently calls for the other as well. Although in pure legal theory it ought not to be the case, since the patent specification ought to contain all the information necessary to enable an invention to be used satisfactorily, the mere licensing of a patent is often of limited value without the associated " know-how," and the imparting of " know-how " frequently requires to be supplemented by the licensing of patents.

It is desirable to review the nature, in law, of a patent, and in so doing to discern some of the peculiarities of this particular form of industrial property, peculiarities which, as will become evident, make it very different in its true nature from any other proprietary right known to the law. The patent laws of most industrial countries [1] are very similar. There are, however, differences in their underlying philosophy due to their different national historical backgrounds, and of more practical importance, differences in the way in which they are administered, so that the possession of an issued patent is likely to be of more true value in, say, Germany or the United States where applications are stringently examined, than in France or Belgium where they are not. In the United Kingdom, which in respect of examination procedures occupies an intermediate position between the two extremes, the whole of the patent law originates from a single section of the Statute of Monopolies 1628. This statute was passed by Parliament in its battle with the Stuarts in order to curb

[1] Excluding, that is to say, the countries of the Communist part of the world, where there are some basic differences of approach.

the exercise by the Crown of the supposed right to grant to individuals as a mark of favour or for valuable consideration, the exclusive right to exercise a particular calling or to market some kind of merchandise in a defined area or for a specified period. The pretended grant of monopolies was deemed to be contrary to public interest and was declared illegal, but in section 6 the statute provided:

> "that any declaration before mentioned [*i.e.* the declaration that monopolies should be void] shall not extend to any letters patent and grants of privilege for the term of fourteen years or under, hereafter to be made, of the sole working or making of any manner of new manufactures within this realm, to the true and first inventor and inventors of such manufactures which other at the time of making such letters patent and grants shall not use ..."

Patent law in the United Kingdom rested upon this slender statutory foundation for more than two hundred years until 1852, when the Patent Office was founded and a system of registration introduced. The expression "true and first invention" still endures and the link with the Statute of Monopolies is maintained in that the word "invention" is still defined [2] as meaning "any manner of new manufacture the subject of letters patent and grant of privilege within section 6 of the Statute of Monopolies." It will be observed that to be patentable an invention must be for manufacture, whether it be a method of manufacture or the article manufactured, or more commonly, both.

The nature of a patent is therefore the monopoly right to engage in a specified manufacturing operation or to deal with a specified manufactured article for the period of the patent (now sixteen years [3] in the United Kingdom). Expressed thus the right seems easy to define, and indeed it is. It is in practice that the complications are found, and unfortunately few businessmen, even in manufacturing industry, make the necessary effort to understand the nature of those complications and to recognise the resulting uncertainties which surround the exercise and enforcement of patent rights. The complications derive principally from the simple fact that to endeavour to prove oneself the

[2] Patents Act 1949, s. 101.
[3] With the possibility of limited extension in special circumstances.

" true and first inventor " is to set out to prove a negative, *viz.* to show that no one previously used or published the same invention. To prove a negative proposition with finality is virtually impossible.

The following is a brief summary of the procedure followed in the application for a patent and between application and ultimate grant.

1. An application is made supported by a " provisional " specification. This establishes a " priority date."

2. Not more than twelve months later a "complete " specification is filed. The complete specification may elaborate the matter contained in the provisional specification, but will not be accorded the priority date of the provisional in respect of any matter not " fairly based " upon the disclosures contained in the provisional specification.

3. During an unspecified period, often extending to some years, the specification is " examined," during which period the official examiner may challenge the novelty of the invention basing his criticisms upon matter contained in other patent specifications filed during the preceding fifty years.

4. When the official examiner is satisfied, the specification is printed and published, and for three months remains open to public opposition. The most frequent ground for opposition is the allegation that there has been prior publication and that the supposed " true and first inventor " was not indeed such.

5. If there is no opposition, or when any opposition is overcome, the patent is sealed, and it is then a granted patent.

These steps usually take at least two years and may occupy a much longer period. Even when they are complete it is still possible for any interested person at any time during the life of the patent to apply for a revocation either by a petition to the court or by way of a defence to an action for infringement and the same facts which would have supported opposition as indicated in (4) above will ground an action for revocation. The discovery, for example, of a reference in an obscure publication even in a foreign language, proved to have been placed on the shelves of a technical library before the priority date, will, if it shows anticipation of the invention, be sufficient to have the patent revoked, if anyone is sufficiently interested to pay the costs and take the initiative involved. It is this fact which causes the possession of patent rights to be beset with uncertainty of a kind not met with in connection with any other type of property. One can be satisfied that one's title to property in land is absolute and unassailable, and within reason the same is true of chattels, but in the last resort *no amount of analysis and searching will ever suffice to guarantee that the validity of a patent will not be successfully assailed.* Often the possession of a published specification which has passed through its three months' opposition period unscathed is regarded by the layman as evidencing his possession of patent rights, and if the possibility of the patent being challenged is drawn to his attention he expects to be able to submit the question " is this patent valid? " to his patent agent and to be assured that it is. It is difficult for him to appreciate that all the technical and legal expertise available cannot do more than justify him in regarding his patent position as *likely* to succeed against attack. The likelihood can never reach certainty. Even a successful defence against an action for revocation in the highest court does not remove the possibility of a fresh attack based on new facts.

The essence of any licence is that it constitutes permission by the licensor for the licensee to do some action which in the absence of the licence would be a tort against the licensor. A patent being a monopoly right, the infringement of the patent, *i.e.* the carrying out of manufacture according to the method described in the patent, by a person other than the patentee, would be a tort, and the licence thus constitutes permission for the period for which it is granted for the licensee to manufacture in accordance with the patent. A licence can therefore be a very simple document, the essential requirements being the identification of the parties, the patent and the term, the formal statement that the licensor grants the licence to the licensee and (unless the licence is free) provision for payment by royalty or otherwise. There is provision at the Patent Office [4] for the registration of licences, which thus become public documents. If a licence is to be registered it must be executed under seal. All licences, however, are not drawn up in this way and to be effective as between the licensor and licensee there is need neither for the formality of sealing nor registration at the Patent Office. The

[4] Under s. 74 of the Patents Act 1949.

difference in law between a licence executed formally and registered and one not registered is, however, considerable. The properly executed and registered licence vests in the licensee rights which cannot be overridden, since any other subsequent purported licensee must be deemed to take his licence subject to and with knowledge of the first licensee's rights, evidenced as they are in a public document. On the other hand, the licensee who takes under an unregistered licence will have no action against a subsequent licensee who takes in good faith and without notice of the first licensee's rights, and if such subsequent licensee takes under a formal and properly registered licence he may be able to sue the first and unregistered licensee for infringement, leaving him only the remedy of suing the licensor for damages. Because of the desirability of registration for the sake of security, and the disadvantage of the attendant publicity, it is therefore not uncommon for a bare licence providing for nominal consideration to be executed and registered, whilst any more elaborate terms which the parties desire to incorporate into the arrangement made between them are simultaneously written into a more detailed agreement which is not placed on the public file. Most of the practical considerations arising in the course of drafting and negotiation are likely to concern this detailed and less formal agreement, and it is to this that the remainder of this portion of the chapter will be directed.

In considering the drafting or examining such an agreement it will be convenient to summarise heads under a threefold classification:

    1. The basic facts.
    2. The interest of the licensor.
    3. The interest of the licensee.

1. The basic facts

These are the same matters as constitute the substance of the formal and registered licence if one is executed.

    (a) First of all, the licence may be exclusive, sole, or non-exclusive. An exclusive licence using the term in the meaning applied to it by the Patents Act 1949 has the effect of vesting in the licensee, for the duration of the licence, the whole of the rights under the patent to the exclusion of the patentee himself. Under such an agreement (assuming that it, or a corresponding formal licence has been placed on the register) the licensee alone will be entitled to sue infringers and will do so in his own name. A sole licence is one that constitutes the licensee the only licensee, but does not preclude the patentee himself from exercising rights under the patent. A non-exclusive licence merely allows the licensee to operate under the patent, leaving it open for the patentee to grant other licences.

(b) The patent or patents must be identified.

(c) The duration of the licence must be stated with the provisions for termination, if so desired.

(d) It must be made clear whether any annuity charges necessary to keep the patent in being are to be paid by the patentee or the licensee.

(e) Any limitation placed on the rights of the licensee to export the patented article should be defined; this depending upon the existence of corresponding foreign patents.

(f) The basis of royalty or other payments must be defined and an arrangement inserted for the time, method, and certification of returns.

(g) Whether there is to be any right to sub-license.

These matters are likely to have been agreed between the parties before detailed drafting of the agreements began, or if not so agreed are not likely to be contentious since they depend upon the factual position. It is when the interests of the two parties are considered in more detail, especially in respect of a line of action to be taken in the event of infringement by a third party, that complications are liable to ensue.

2. The interest of the licensor

(a) The principal interest of the licensor is to obtain remuneration from the licensee, and to do this it is necessary, especially in the case of an exclusive or sole licensee (since his shortcomings cannot be overcome by the appointment of additional licensees) for the obligation to be laid upon him to operate the patent to the best of his ability and to foster the business to which the patent relates. It may be possible to lay down some criterion by way of a minimum turnover, failure to attain which will permit the termination of the licence, or its conversion into a non-exclusive licence.

(b) In order to be assured of the bona fides of the operation of the licence the licensor should reserve some rights of examination of the licensee's books, or, alternatively, the right to call for audited statements supporting payment of royalties, the dates for payment of which should be specified.

(c) It is not unusual for the licensor (normally, of course, the patentee) to require the licensee to acknowledge expressly that all the claims in the licensed patents are valid, and to give an undertaking that he will not contest them.

(d) If the licensee is the party whose duty it is to pay annuities for the renewal of the patent the licensor should secure the right to have evidence produced that they have been paid, and in default to be entitled himself to pay them and recover from the licensee.

(e) It may sometimes happen that in the course of operating a patent the licensee may originate further inventions that will provide the basis for improvements, or may constitute alternative methods of working taking the operation outside the scope of the patent. The interest of the licensor in the case of improvements is to have the licensee disclose them and (if the patentee is active in the business and has not divested himself of his rights by granting an exclusive licence) either to permit the licensor to apply for patents in respect of the improvements or himself to apply and to cross-license the licensor freely under them. In the case of alternative methods which come to light enabling the patent to be by-passed, the interest of the licensor is so to word the agreement that the royalty is applied to operations of that kind equally with those properly under the patent. This of course, takes the agreement beyond the scope of a patent licence proper.

(f)   It is in the interest of the licensor that he should not be placed under the obligation to undertake litigation against an infringer, but should be able to exercise a power of choice. Patent litigation is notoriously expensive and uncertain, and since the inevitable answer to an action for infringement includes a claim for revocation of the patent, the patentee is ill advised to commence an action unless (i) he is reasonably certain of success (as has been said, he can never be quite certain), and (ii) the infringement is on such a scale and sufficiently flagrant to justify the expense. The licensor will therefore call upon the licensee to advise him promptly of any infringement coming to the licensor's knowledge but will try to escape being placed under obligation to commence proceedings against an infringer against his better judgment.

3. The interest of the licensee

It is clear that in a number of respects the interests of the licensor set out in the foregoing paragraphs are directly opposed to the interests of the licensee, as to which:

(a)   The licensee's primary interest is to obtain, in return for his payment of royalties, protection sufficiently real to justify the expense. To him, the whole essence of the contract is that he must be assured that by comparison with any person (other than a co-licensee in the case of a non-exclusive licence) he has a tangible advantage to compensate for loading his manufacturing costs with the royalty or other payment which he is required to make to the licensor.

(b)   It is in the interest of the licensee, therefore, that if any infringement occurs, it will be dealt with by the patentee. He will therefore wish, contrary to the desire of the licensor (see paragraph (f) above) to have an obligation laid upon the licensor to sue any infringer.

(c)   It is against the interest of the licensee to yield the admissions which are likely to be called for by the licensor ((c) above) regarding the validity of the claims under the patent, since such an admission could seriously hamper him if he were to find himself in dispute with the licensor.

(d) If the licensor is the party liable to keep the patent in being by the payment of annuities, the licensee should in his own interest secure the right to make payments in default of the licensor to recover.

It is clear from the foregoing that in any discussions between the proposed licensor and the licensee in which a serious attempt is being made by each party to understand and to meet the reasonable requirements of the other a real quandary is met with when consideration is given to the course of action to be taken in the case of infringement occurring on a significant scale. The licensee, if he is wise, will not place himself in a position in which he will have to load a royalty charge into his manufacturing costs, while a competitor may be allowed to infringe with impunity and thus obtain an advantage in costs. He must have some assurance in the matter, and yet the licensor, for his own part, cannot reasonably be expected to undertake what could be vexatious and disastrously expensive litigation in circumstances which do not justify it.

This quandary is sometimes evaded by the unsound device of "agreeing to agree." A clause is written round the formula that in the event of the licensee complaining of infringement the parties will confer with a view to reaching agreement as to the course to be taken. This arrangement often proves satisfactory in action; whilst it is really an evasion of the difficulty it has the advantage of frankly recognising that only in the precise circumstances in which the infringement occurs can a sound decision be taken as to whether to sue. Other possible methods of providing for the circumstances are:

(a) The licensor may be called upon to take action with the proviso that he need not do so if the infringement is not so substantial as to constitute a serious threat to the licensee's interests. What level of activity would be substantial would be a matter of fact to be decided by arbitration or by the court in the light of circumstances.

(b) The licensee may be placed by the agreement under obligation to pay some part of the costs of litigation, thus rendering it unlikely that he will demand action frivolously.

(c) A provision may be introduced into the agreement providing for its termination in the event of the licensor being unwilling to act against a substantial infringer. Such a clause needs to be carefully worded to provide against the licensee using it to obtain the right to terminate the agreement by means of an artificially contrived situation.

(d) The licensor may be given the option of either suing the infringer or reducing the level of royalty payments.

(e) Recourse may be had to arbitration.

(f) Provision may be made that the licensor should not be required to undertake any action if in the opinion of patent counsel success is unlikely.

The foregoing compromises are not intended as exhaustive, and indeed many others have been worked out. They are designed to illustrate the manner in which the quandary may be approached. If the patent is successfully challenged in the courts and is revoked, or is allowed to lapse, the Patents Act 1949 itself provides a way out for the licensee, notwithstanding anything that he may have accepted in the agreement regarding the validity of the claims in the licensed patent. Section 58 provides that:

" any contract . . . for licence to manufacture, use or work a patented article or process . . . may at any time after the patent or all the patents by which the article or process was protected at the time of the making of the contract has or have ceased to be in force, and notwithstanding anything to the contrary in the contract or in any other contract, be determined by either party on giving three months' notice in writing to the other party."

It is to deal with a situation short of the patent ceasing to be in force, the situation in which it is still on the register but is not giving protection to the licensee, that the parties have to deal. It is because the problem is to deal with a situation which has practical reality but is not recognisable by the law that it cannot be provided with a neat contractual procedure.

Because of the technical background against which they arise
in practice, agreements for the sale of " know-how " are often
linked with patent licensing arrangements and are sometimes
dealt with in the same document.[5]   If the agreement for the sale
or licensing of patent rights is complicated by special difficulties
because of the inherent difficulty in judging the strength of any
patent, the agreement for the sale of knowledge is even more
complicated in that it consists of the sale of something that is
neither real property, nor chattel, nor resting in definable legally
enforceable rights, something indeed whose nature cannot, at the
time the agreement is entered into, be described in detail at all.
Commonly, the situation is one in which an undertaking or a
person is recognised as being in possession of expert knowledge
or experience, normally in manufacturing industry or in technology.
It is natural that, to some degree, it or he may have taken
advantage of the patent law to obtain protection of some aspects
of his expertise, where it can be identified as a specific invention.
There is, however, a wide gulf between the theory of inventions and
their protection as envisaged by the law and the actual progress
of technical advance in real life.   In the legal view inventions are
individual and capable of specification, made by individual
inventors who can and will describe them in specifications
clear enough to enable any other person possessing a general
background knowledge of the industry concerned (in legal words
" skilled in the art ") to use them if he is legally empowered to
do so either by licence or by the lapsing of the patent.   In
practice, technological advance takes place on a broad front as a
result of research teams co-operating with those concerned with
practical product development and with observers in the field.
In the active organisation there is frequent experiment involving
changes of design and experience is gradually accumulated.   When
a new product is introduced its teething troubles will be investigated and corrected and by this means an increasing fund of
knowledge comes into being.

The sale of " know-how " is the method by which, for valuable
consideration, the technical knowledge and practical experience of
one undertaking is placed at the disposal of another.   It is a
much wider and surer arrangement than patent licensing, and it

[5] It has been argued that this is undesirable partly because of the provisions of
s. 58 of the Patents Act 1949 and also for tax reasons.

would be generally agreed that the intangible "know-how," involving guidance in dealing with difficulties in practical information regarding materials, specifications, and the like is frequently far more important and valuable than any patents incidentally involved.

The draftsman of a "know-how" agreement can avail himself of tried precedents,[6] but to an extent greater than that applicable to most agreements, the lawyer must, and is entitled to, look to the business client for assistance, for in all the technical aspects of the matter he is the layman and the client the expert. The normal content of a "know-how" agreement between an experienced manufacturing organisation and an inexperienced manufacturer, frequently in another country, who wishes to enter a field of manufacture strange to him, will be based upon and include the following:

   (a) The making available of initial information, including drawings, technical data, materials, specifications, manufacturing methods, designs of tools, and the like. This may in some circumstances extend to a complete factory lay-out design and assistance in control, recruitment of technical staff, etc.

   (b) The training of technicians and key workers.

   (c) A service of technical advice on difficulties encountered, and on new developments made.

   (d) The licensing of the purchaser under any patents necessary to the manufacture.

   (e) The use of trademarks, trade names, and the like.

The principal interest of the receiving party in any such agreement is to be fully assured that he will get what he bargains for, and that the selling party will not conceal or hold back from him any information that is relevant. His first concern will therefore be that he shall feel a genuine trust in the seller's good faith, and this will be matched by care to ensure that the contract is so worded as to entitle him to *all* the available information as he needs it and to enable him to challenge the seller in the courts if he finds that there is any reticence on his part.

The principal interests of the seller of "know-how" are:

---

[6] *e.g. Agreement for the Sale of " Know-how,"* T. A. Blanco White (Sweet & Maxwell, 1962).

(a) To be sure that the buyer will in fact use the " know-how " properly, so that any consideration related to output or sales will be adequate. He will therefore wish to provide for substantial initial payment and for subsequent minimum sums.

(b) To ensure that information given in confidence will be treated as confidential. To this end he will be well advised to retain copyright in drawings and other documents and require that they be delivered up at the end of the agreement.

It is upon this last point that some of the most elusive difficulties arise. A licence once granted can be revoked if circumstances so justify, but knowledge once imparted cannot be withdrawn. Further, all knowledge vests ultimately in individuals, many or all of whom are not privy to the contract, and are not bound thereunder. Even if the item of knowledge imparted in confidence can be identified, it is not likely to be possible to restrain any person from acting on what he knows.[7] The technician who knows that it is best for part X to be fabricated in alloy A and transfers to new employment is not likely deliberately to manufacture it in some other material because the knowledge reached him as a result of his former employer gaining it under a " know-how " agreement.

Thus, just as the practical problem in the patent licence is what to do in the case of infringement, the practical problem in the sale of " know-how " is what to do to prevent leaks of information. It is difficult to draw an agreement in the interest of the seller without rendering it in the last resort incapable of operation. Thus a form sometimes used [8] provides:

B [the buyer] undertakes that information . . . shall not at any time be disclosed by any person who has received the same from . . . B except . . . to a responsible employee of B.

B further undertakes that such information shall not *at any time* be used . . . by any such person as aforesaid for the purposes . . . of this agreement.

[7] Although this was attempted in *Cranleigh Precision Engineering* v. *Bryant* [1964] 3 All E.R. 289.

[8] Blanco-White, *op. cit.*

To expect to control the use of factual knowledge within the mind of an employee who has ceased to be an employee is to cry for the moon, and it is not wise for the buyer of "know-how" to promise more than that he will use all reasonable precautions to prevent or control the dissemination of trade secrets, and with such a promise the seller must be content, for nothing more can be effectively promised.

CHAPTER 9

"AGENCIES" AND DISTRIBUTOR AGREEMENTS

THERE are certain words which, in the mouth of a lawyer, possess a special and precise meaning different from that which they possess in ordinary parlance and perhaps the best possible example of this is the word "agent." There are a number of relationships known to the law in which one party is "agent" of another as his "principal." There are a number of typical relationships known to industry and commerce in which one undertaking will hold itself out as "agent" for this or that. Those two classes of relationship are by no means the same, and this chapter is concerned with a class of contract determining the rights and liabilities of the parties in those relationships which are called "agency" in the commercial rather than the legal meaning of the word.

The difference, however, between the legal meaning and the commercial meaning of the word "agent" is so important, and so inadequately understood in the commerical world that it is worthy of some comment before proceeding to consider the content of the typical commercial agency agreement. "Agency," according to a standard textbook,[1] "is the relationship which exists between two persons, one of whom, the principal, expressly or implicitly consents that the other, the agent, similarly consenting, should represent him or act on his behalf." The nature of the relationship of agency is therefore that as a result of the act of an agent, performed within his proper authority, a contractual relationship can be created between the principal, for whom the agent has acted, and the third party with whom the agent, on behalf of the principal, has acted. Once that contractual relationship has been established that agent is himself no party to it. He may and does owe duties to the principal and to the other contracting party, but those duties do not themselves arise under the contract which, by his agency, he has brought into being. A typical example of true agency in operation is when an auctioneer who

---

[1] *Bowstead on Agency* (12th ed.), p. 1.

has been entrusted with goods or property for sale duly sells them by auction. The vendor cannot refuse to be bound by the contract, and at the fall of the hammer that contract is created between the vendor and the purchaser. Now it is quite clear that this sort of relationship, of which many examples could be quoted, is very different from the relationships which exist between manufacturers and those of their distributors who declare themselves to be " agents for X's bicycles " or who are described by the manufacturers as being " sole agents " for a specified territory.

It is perhaps because the common word " agent " is not strictly applicable that a number of other words are sometimes used to describe the arrangements envisaged in these agreements. " Distributor " is perhaps the most frequently used, " Concessionaire " is also met with. One often hears the word " franchise " applied, perhaps not very accurately, to the right granted to deal in the goods of a particular manufacturer. There is no particular magic in any of these terms; they are largely synonymous and if there are shades of difference of meaning they are not easily defined. One sound reason for avoiding the use of the word " agent " appears when the arrangement is concerned with the distribution of a manufacturer's goods in overseas countries. Many countries have income tax laws narrowly drawn to render liable to tax any person or company " trading " within the country even though not domiciled there, and the possession of an " agent " in a country is liable to be taken as prima facie evidence that the principal trades within the country. If it is desired to establish that all sales by the principal take place before the goods reach the country, as for example when goods are shipped f.o.b. United Kingdom port, it is best to avoid the word " agent " in the agreement.

Basically, there is no need for any agreement to exist for the distribution of goods within a market to take place. There is no intrinsic reason why a manufacturer should not sell his goods to any purchaser, leaving them to find their way to the ultimate user by normal and uncontrolled sales through the market. Alternatively, it is possible for a manufacturer to sell his entire output to a wholesaler who then organises distribution, relieving the manufacturer of this aspect of the business. However, it is customary for a manufacturer of any size, especially if his products are of a nature to call for after-sales service, to wish to exercise some general control over the pattern of his selling, to secure that he has sales outlets at all the most significant available points, and at the same time, to secure that his sales agents (using the term in the colloquial and non-technical sense) will participate in an arrangement sufficiently attractive to give them an incentive in furthering sales and satisfying the ultimate user.

It is most usual for the manufacturer to take the initiative in seeking sales agents, although conversely it is in the interest of the distributor to build up a suitably complementary collection of products. The nature of the product, however, must naturally affect the detail of the agreement, and for this reason it is natural that the manufacturer should create the form of the agreement. Further, although it is by no means always the case, the manufacturer is most often in the position of a greater economic strength, the distributor's business being local and relatively smaller, so that the manufacturer tends to dictate the form of the agreement. When the position is reversed, as for example when a powerful distribution organisation such as a chain store system take up the products of a small manufacturer, the tendency is for it to demand complete freedom in the method of handling, so that an agency agreement is irrelevant or superfluous.

The typical situation with which this chapter is concerned is therefore one in which the manufacturer of products of such a nature as to require an after-sales service and to render desirable some regulated source of technical information, is arranging for a system of sales outlets to cover all available markets. Since such a general situation is capable of almost infinite variation, and since the products included in the description could range from entire chemical engineering plants to safety razors, the agreements will themselves be of widely different kinds. Even so, however, they will tend to possess a family likeness.

It is clear that this type of organised marketing system as applied to technical products is of increasing importance in the total economic picture. The old picture of commercial life was concerned with buying and selling, the merchant holding stocks and using his knowledge of commodities to buy wisely and sell profitably, building his own reputation and goodwill upon his personal judgment of goods. Though there is still room for this kind of merchanting skill, the class of commodities to which this kind of marketing can be applied forms a decreasing proportion of the total volume of trade. Today the old style merchant has largely given place to the distributive organisation, and a retailer's personal judgments are of less practical significance than reputations built into the goods by nation-wide and even world-wide publicity. For this reason the agreement regulating distributorship is becoming of increasing significance.

Before framing agreements of this kind, there are certain basic decisions to be taken with regard to the pattern of trading which it is intended to foster. Fundamentally, " distributors " or " agents " are of two kinds, those who buy and resell as principals, and those who are concerned only to collect orders for the principal, so that the ultimate sale takes place from the manufacturer to the customer. It is necessary to keep this distinction clearly in mind, especially when, as sometimes happens, a " distributor " or " agent " who represents a manufacturer in respect of a number of products may handle some in one way and some in the other. In general, the principal-to-principal basis of distributorship is likely to apply in the case of small products of which the unit cost is manageable in the normal course of business and of which stocks are held, whereas the arrangement in which the " agent " acts as the eyes and ears of the manufacturer, seeking essentially to be no more than the liaison between the manufacturer and the customer, is likely to apply in respect of products of greater technical complexity and higher unit cost.

As has been pointed out, in the home market a considerable proportion of the materials of commerce find their way from manufacturer to user through the ordinary unregulated operations of the market. The distributorship agreement becomes of importance especially where the products are technical or where they are branded goods nationally advertised. To a considerable degree, such products sell themselves, and the manufacturer can use the strength of the brand to persuade the selling outlet, whether retail or wholesale, to sign an agreement in standard form whereby he is able to keep a degree of control over the structure of the distributive system for his products.

The following are the topics most likely to be contained in the agreement:

(a) The retailer or wholesaler is appointed as distributor, with the appropriate status. At this point it is necessary to be clear whether the distributorship is exclusive on a territorial basis. Without some undertaking on the part of the manufacturer not to appoint other distributors for the same products in the same district the agreement is obviously of very limited value. In the case of agreements relating to the distribution of products otherwise than by retail sale, a distinction must be made between an exclusive appointment as distributor, in the sense of the distributor being the only one appointed in a given area, and an undertaking that the area will be exclusively reserved to the distributor. Thus a manufacturer may agree to appoint a distributor in Essex and one in Suffolk, each being assured that no other distributor will be appointed in his own county, whilst each distributor may be free to sell wherever he is able and willing to do so. Thus there will be active competition between various distributors. Such an arrangement accords better with the internal marketing freedom expected by purchasers in a home market than an attempt to give a monopoly of a given territory to one distributor, entailing, as it does, a restraint against his dealing with customers outside his territory. The important point to observe, however, is that the agreement must be quite definite in showing what degree of exclusiveness, if any, is conferred, and if the activity of a distributor is restricted to a defined territory there should be a related undertaking by the manufacturer to place corresponding restrictions on others.

(b) If the products are such that customers are likely to seek to deal with the manufacturer direct it is desirable for the agreement to make clear what degree of liberty the manufacturer retains in this matter. It is not uncommon for a manufacturer to reserve the right to deal with customers direct but to pay a commission in such cases to the distributor in whose territory the customer is situate. In any such case and also when any exclusive territorial rights are being conferred, it is important to be quite clear by what criterion the location of a customer is to be determined. It is possible for the registered office of a company, the administrative office from which the orders are placed, the commercial office at which decisions are taken, and the location where goods are to be used, all to be at different points, and this can lead to serious dispute if the question arises which of a number of distributors with territorial rights is to benefit from a sale.

(c) If the manufacturer does not wish to reserve the right to deal with customers direct it is proper to provide for inquiries from the distributor's territory received by him to be referred to the distributor.

(d) In some cases it is proper to provide that the distributor will not deal in goods of a nature to compete with those covered by the agreement. This, in the last resort, is a matter of commercial expediency and negotiation. In the retail trade it is less appropriate than in the case of the distribution of technical products.

(e) Where the distributorship is based on a principal-to-principal relationship, and the distributor buys goods from the manufacturer for sale in his own name to resell on his own account, it is usual for a distributorship agreement, except where goods are of high value or are of a nature to be custom built, to require the distributor to carry adequate stocks of the goods. Without such a provision the agreement is of little value to the manufacturer, since no obligation rests upon the distributor, who may remain quite inactive. In the case of consumer goods the vital need to the manufacturer is for them to be in the market place, and the requirement for the distributor to hold a minimum stock is the first step on the way from factory to ultimate user. This arrangement can be furthered by various devices aimed at assisting the distributor in the stockholding function. It may be done quite simply by giving an extended credit so that in the normal course of trade goods are sold by the distributor by the time when he has to pay for them. Other more elaborate methods are the holding of goods by the distributor on a consignment stock or accommodation stock basis. Under these arrangements the goods remain the property of the manufacturer until disposed of by the distributor, who is deemed to have bought them simultaneously with his sale to his own customer. When these arrangements are entered into it is important for the agreement to be precise in making clear whether an ultimate obligation rests upon the distributor to purchase the goods at some definable date whether or not he has disposed of them, or, on the other hand, whether he is entitled in default of sale to return them. The last-mentioned arrangement is a dangerous one to the manufacturer, as there can be few more embarrassing situations than to have a quantity of obsolete and possibly unsaleable stock returned to the factory.

(f) The agreement will provide for the detailed conditions of sale which are to apply as between manufacturer and distributor. They may be included in full or incorporated by reference. There is advantage in the latter course, and if it is followed the agreement should be so worded as to incorporate the standard conditions as effective from time to time.   Otherwise it is possible to find that after conditions of sale have been revised for valid reasons the old conditions will continue to apply in the case of sales to all distributors with agreements incorporating the obsolete conditions.

(g) Together with conditions of sale, and more practically important, terms of payment must be dealt with.   This is bound up with the general and broad principle of the burden of stock financing, as has already been indicated.

(h) In the case of all technical products, the matter of after-sales service and guarantee call for attention.   It is necessary to be clear as to the distribution of responsibility for (i) free repairs under guarantee, and (ii) normal repair service as between the manufacturer and the distributor. Where a manufacturer possesses an overall service department the distributor may be relieved of responsibility, but even so it is desirable to lay upon him a definite obligation to forward complaints promptly and perhaps to make preliminary investigations.   In other cases more definite obligations may rest upon the distributor.

(j) It is sometimes the practice for a contribution to the cost of local advertising to be made by the manufacturer to the distributor and for the basis of such a contribution to be provided for in the agreement.   Correspondingly it may be desirable for the manufacturer to undertake to support the distributor by national advertising.

(k) Sometimes, especially where goods are such as to confer prestige upon the distributor, it is the practice to place upon him the onus of maintaining a defined level of business.   This obligation is capable of being expressed in different ways, and perhaps the most just and practical is for the basic general obligation resting upon the distributor to be that of using all reasonable efforts to foster the business, coupled with the right on the part of the manufacturer to terminate the distributorship if the obligation is not performed, the whole arrangement being coupled with a rider that provided the business transacted in any year amounts to £X the obligation will be deemed to be performed. The virtue of such an arrangement is that the distributor knows that his continuance as a distributor is safe if he maintains the specified turnover, whilst if he falls below the datum it becomes a question of fact whether he has fulfilled his obligation to use reasonable efforts. The manufacturer knows that a datum is established and if it is not reached he has the right to make inquiries, but there is no suggestion that he is making the agreement into a dead letter if he takes no action to terminate it for reasons of general bad trade or if otherwise there is justifiable reason for the shortfall.

(l) The distributor has a right to be assured that if he is to be in competition with other distributors he will not be put at a disadvantage by their being given better terms than he is himself. It is therefore usual to provide for a specified discount from list prices to apply, or sometimes in general terms for the distributor to have the benefit of "preferential prices and discounts." This phrase is generally understood in business, notwithstanding its legal imprecision, as having the effect of entitling the distributor to equal treatment with others.

(m) In the past it has been usual to require distributors to undertake specific liabilities in the matter of maintaining standard prices and, in the event of their standing in the position of wholesalers or main distributors, a standard discount structure in the further stages of distribution. By the Resale Prices Act 1964 the inclusion of any such provision has become unlawful and its effect in existing contracts avoided. Control of resale prices can now be exercised in respect only of goods exempted from the operation of the Act by the Restrictive Practices Court.

(n) The agreement should be entered into for a specified minimum term and be terminable thereafter by specified notice. The usual provisions for summary termination in the event of insolvency or breach should be provided.

In the foregoing suggested topics for inclusion in a distributorship agreement, the home market has been in mind. Many of the provisions are equally applicable to the case of an agreement for overseas distribution, but there are certain differences of emphasis when the distributor is in a different country from the manufacturer. It is customary for the overseas distributor to take much more initiative, to stand in a position of greater independence. The practice of giving one undertaking exclusive rights of representation in a territory is more general, and such an undertaking will have the right in appropriate circumstances of appointing sub-distributors and organising the system of distribution throughout the territory.

In the case of technical products the acquisition by a manufacturer of an efficient foreign or overseas distributor is much more vital because of the need for servicing of the products, and the selection of overseas distributors is largely dominated by the need to give adequate after-sales service. In many countries, especially those where development is as yet only partial, it is easy to find many would-be distributors, especially if the manufacturer is not exacting in the matter of stockholding, and many such " distributors " love to amass an imposing array of manufacturers for whom they are " agents " but for whom they do very little. It is a different matter to find one who is able to support his distributorship with an efficient after-sales service.

For this reason the emphasis upon a minimum level of business becomes more significant, and it is usual to require the distributor to show evidence of his activity in giving proper publicity to the products within his own territory.

In the case of products which are normally sold from stock, the maintenance of adequate stocks in the territory becomes of great importance, and it is in the development of overseas markets that it can become particularly important to develop arrangements for the financing of stocks by consignment or accommodation stock arrangements.

In the framing of the type of " agency " agreement where the function of the agent is merely to be the eyes and ears of the manufacturer, to be a channel for the passing of information to and from potential customers, and to negotiate contracts to which when established he will not himself be a party, considerably less detail is called for. It is usual for such an agent to be remunerated by a commission on the sales effected as a result of his activities. It is necessary, however, to be very clear as to the degree of freedom to be retained by the manufacturer in dealing direct with inquiries emanating from the territory. It is easy for him to find himself, as a result of the imprecise wording of an agreement, under obligation to pay substantial commissions to an agent who has taken no real initiative. In the interest of the agent, however, and in fairness to him, it is important to secure that he shall not be denied the right to receive commission merely because the ultimate order placed by the customer does not pass through his hands, when he may have been active in the liaison that led to the inquiry being made, or may be left with obligations in respect of the servicing of products. Because of the infinite diversity of the circumstances surrounding various industries it is not possible to suggest any general method of treating this problem, but the course of wisdom is to consider all the possible foreseeable variants at the time when the agreement is drafted.

No excellence in the drafting of agreements can turn bad representation into good, and the selection of good representation in the sales field, whether at home or abroad, is one of the principal factors of success in manufacturing industry, second indeed only to having a technically adequate product. The agreement should, however, be tailored to the needs of the parties, and if it is well and fairly drawn it will be such as to entitle each party to the satisfaction of its legitimate rights. These can be expressed very simply.

The needs of the manufacturer are:

(a) To have his goods offered to the public through channels of distribution which are adequate in every way: in the dissemination of information, the satisfaction of inquiries and the transmission of requests for specific requirements, in the holding of proper stocks and their display.

(b) To have proper after-sales service given to users of his goods, and, if this is a function which he performs himself, to be sure that an adequate channel for the transmission of complaints is kept open and properly used, and that his own image in the user's mind is kept bright.

(c) To be paid for his goods and his services at the right time.

The interests of the distributor are almost as simply expressed:

(a) To have a product to offer which is technically

adequate and to know that it will be kept up to date with technical progress in the industry.

(b) To have a proper and adequate flow of information.

(c) To be able to offer to customers the assurance of proper after-sales service.

(d) To have support in the form of publicity.

(e) To be protected from unfair competition.

The draftsman of the distributorship agreement will do well to keep these few simple expectations on both sides in mind: if he does, the agreement he produces will not be impractical or unfair.

CHAPTER 10

WRITING THE COMMERCIAL AGREEMENT

HOWEVER carefully one may provide oneself with standard forms of agreement, with conditions of sale and purchase and the like, to meet all the typical situations which one expects to occur in the course of business, sooner or later a situation is sure to arise which calls for the formulation of an agreement for which no neat precedent is available. When this happens there is nothing to be done but to take pen in hand and to write the agreement for oneself or, alternatively, to go to the professional lawyers and ask them to do the same. The decision whether to make use of the services of professional lawyers is one of the first to present itself, and whilst either way the decision may be the right one, it is important that it be taken for the right reason. As was suggested earlier in this book, there is in every business a point at which the solicitors are bound to be involved, and there is another point at which the transactions of the business are so frequent and so casual that, except for the possibility of general precautions it is not possible to consider each transaction in its legal and contractual background, although one knows that it exists. Between these two points lie a variety of transactions having legal effects and in relationship to which someone in the organisation must exercise what in the opening chapter was called " the legal function." The question whether to consult the solicitors when an *ad hoc* situation presents itself demanding a specially formulated agreement is essentially the question where the upper of those limiting points is to be fixed.

There are certain factors which are valid in the decision. If the agreement is one which is to regulate a situation in which litigation is seen to be a not remote possibility, it is not only foolish not to consult one's solicitors but also unfair to them, since if litigation takes place they will have to interpret the agreement and claim their client's rights thereunder, and they ought to have been given an opportunity to take a hand in framing it in the first place. There is room here for a sense of proportion and reasonable judgment. There is no situation that

183

cannot in some way lead to the possibility of litigation, for by the very nature of things a contract is an agreement that is capable of being the ground of an action.   But experience leads one to a sense by which certain relationships are seen as most unlikely ever to become sour to the point of litigation, whereas other relationships and situations are, by their very nature, such that from the beginning a realisation is present that they need to be handled with the knowledge that one day they may be examined in the courts.   It is in these latter cases that the course of wisdom is to allow the solicitors to advise and to draft documents at the beginning.   One can only use a reasonable judgment in such matters, realising that one will not always be right.

The next and practical criterion by which the decision is to be taken is the adequacy of one's own resources.   Who, in the business, exercises " the legal function "?   Is he competent? There is a tendency at the present time for the hard line between the calling of the merchant or industrialist and that of the lawyer to become blurred.   Many men trained to the law go into active business, and many men trained for business study the law in greater or lesser detail.   There is, therefore, a very simple question to be faced here and faced honestly, the question whether the drafting of the agreement is within one's capacity.

Legal training consists, on the one hand, of the accumulation of knowledge of statute and of common law principles, but on the other, it is an education in clear thinking.   Clear thinking, however, is no prerogative of the lawyer and in assessing the adequacy of one's resources for bringing into being a new and specially drawn contract the real question is whether one can think sufficiently clearly and express one's thought with precision. One of the most valid reasons for writing one's own agreements by direct contact with the other party or parties, provided there is the readiness and ability to think clearly and write precisely, is that to do so preserves direct contact and the resultant agreement is more likely to represent the meeting of the parties' minds than if it has been distilled through two firms of solicitors.

So there are good and valid reasons for writing one's own agreement in co-operation with the other side.   There are also, however, reasons that are invalid, and if in honesty one recognises that one is being swayed by the wrong motives, the time has come to clear one's mind and, perhaps, take a contrary decision.

One of these invalid reasons is a desire to avoid the use of what is popularly called " legal jargon." Now it is perfectly true that lawyers are sometimes guilty of writing jargon. It is equally true that businessmen are even more frequently guilty of this literary sin. The difference is usually that lawyers' jargon most often consists in the use of expressions hallowed by long usage which are unfamiliar in ordinary speech but which possess the advantage of having a precise meaning. In a little monograph originally written for departmental circulation in the civil service but which became a classic,[1] Sir Ernest Gowers showed how the function of legal language was to remove the " penumbra of ambiguity " which surrounds many of our words. The jargon of businessmen, however, tends in the opposite direction, avoiding precision and substituting mellifluous woolliness for precise statement and creating an all-inclusive " penumbra." One must be very clear in one's own mind why one wishes to " avoid legal jargon." If the intention can be expressed with complete precision in language which is not recognisably the product of legal training, no modern lawyer will object to it, especially if the client emphasises his wishes in this regard. If, however, the desire is only to substitute business jargon for lawyers' jargon it is not a valid reason to exclude the lawyers from the task of draftsmanship.

Another invalid reason for writing one's own agreement to the exclusion of the lawyers is that one may be impatient of legal precision. But the function of an agreement is to express the agreed rights and liabilities of the parties with such precision that there can be no doubt at a future date as to what they are. If the feeling is that to invite one's solicitor to draft an agreement is to cause him to ask a lot of questions and raise many objections, it is a sure sign that the critical attention of a clear mind is a real need in the situation that has called for the agreement to be written. Indeed, it is found in practice that one of the immediate effects of attempting to reduce to writing in a single document an agreement already reached in principle by correspondence and discussion is to show where the thought of the parties is still imprecise. It immediately throws up a crop of questions. " What is to happen if . . . ? " and " suppose the parties fail to agree . . .? "

[1] *Plain Words.*

This latter question is important to ask in respect of any matter in respect of which the agreement calls for later discussion between the parties. Because the agreement which depends for its certainty upon a future agreement may prove to be without effect when that future agreement cannot be reached, it is sometimes provided that, in the event of failure to reach agreement in the future, arbitration shall be invoked. It is necessary to remember in such a case that an arbitrator must be given some criteria upon which to base his decision.

If it is decided that the writing of the agreement is a matter to be properly entrusted to the professional lawyers it must be remembered that the success of the operation still depends upon proper liaison with them. They must be properly briefed, and all the intended content of the proposed agreement made known to them. They will, one might be sure, come back with questions arising from the uncertainties which are thrown up in the operation of drafting. It cannot be too clearly stated, however, that in this matter the responsibility of the lawyers is with the form and perhaps with the legality of the content, whilst the substance of the agreement is a matter for the client.

Even where the professional lawyers are to be engaged, there is value sometimes in writing a first draft oneself, simply because of the way in which the very effort of writing acts as a clarification of one's thought, but also because this is the best way in which to be sure that the matter which it is intended to include is indeed brought to the attention of the professional draftsman.

When all is said, however, there is nothing sacred about the form of a commercial agreement. The idea is often met that because the matters contained in some business arrangement are written in numbered paragraphs, typed on engrossing paper, and tied up with green tape, they have because of this become in some way more binding than if they had been contained in an exchange of correspondence. This is not so. Form is merely a matter of convenience and expediency. Its main advantage is that of precision. As a rule of interpretation it is generally presumed that when the parties to an agreement have distilled the essentials from a prolonged negotiation, arranged them in clearly written and numbered paragraphs, and placed their signatures to the document, the result of their efforts will constitute the whole agreement written between them, and reference to other documents and to correspondence will only be admissible in order to explain any ambiguities or to provide an interpretation of doubtful terms. Thus the "agreement" has much to commend it for the sake of certainty and convenience. This advantage carries a corresponding caveat, in that it is particularly important to be sure that everything which should be included has indeed been included.

From this point forward all that is necessary is clear thought and clear language. The two go together and help each other. The layman writing an agreement should avoid quasi- or pseudo-legal language, and express himself with the utmost clarity of which he is capable. There is a conventional structure for an agreement, which, whilst not having any magic quality, is a matter of convenience. The agreement will commence with a preamble, which sets out the names of the parties, the date of the agreement, and may include an indication of the nature of the agreement, thus:

> This Licence Agreement made the — day of — 19— between X of AB (hereinafter called the Licensor) and Y of CD (hereinafter called the Licensee).

Then will follow the Recitals, the purpose of which is to place the agreement into the context of previous history and relate it with other agreements which may be concerned with the same matters. The Recitals normally commence with the word "Whereas." They do not form part of the agreement proper, but when it is remembered that an agreement may have to be interpreted a number of years after it has been written by persons who had no hand in the writing or negotiation it will be recognised that there is often value in using them to sketch the background circumstances. Thus, for example,

> Whereas:
>
> 1. *Alpha* are in possession of certain valuable information relating to *gammas* and their manufacture and use, and expect in the future to come into possession of further such information.
>
> 2. The parties hereto have agreed that *Alpha* shall assist *Beta*, by making such information available to *Beta* and otherwise, upon the terms and conditions hereinafter set

out, to establish within the United Kingdom a plant for the making of *gammas*.

3. It is the intention of the parties hereto that *gammas* made in the said plant shall be sold and used within the following area (hereinafter called " the territory ") that is to say: . . .

4. It is further the intention of the parties that (unless and until *Alpha* otherwise require) such *gammas* may be sold and used within the following further area (hereinafter called " the additional territory ") that is to say: . . .[2]

If it is necessary for the existence of other agreements to be known of in order that the agreement may be properly interpreted they will be referred to in the Recitals.

The substantive part of the agreement will now follow, in numbered paragraphs. Sometimes, in the case of a lengthy agreement a double numbering system is used, which can be in many forms. A combination of numbers and letters is the most usual: 1 (a) (b) (c), 2 (a) (b) (c), etc., or a double numbering system as used in Acts of Parliament: 1 (1) (2) (3), 2 (1) (2) (3). Sometimes a lengthy agreement will be written in several main sections headed by Roman numerals and subdivided into numbered paragraphs. These are all matters for convenience and the exercise of personal taste.

After the substantive part of the agreement will come the subscriptions. The use of a company seal is becoming less and less customary, and the types of agreement where it is necessary are now few.[3] For most purposes it is enough to have the signature of the appropriate officer of a company. A commercial agreement executed under hand and not affecting the assignment or conveyance of any property should be stamped, and this can be by the use of an adhesive stamp cancelled by the signature of the first party signing the document. There is some value, however, instead of using an adhesive stamp, in applying within thirty days for the document to be stamped by an impressed stamp, because if it does come within one of the categories of document which need a higher value of stamp the fact will then be brought to light.

[2] From precedent in *Agreement for the Sale of " Know-How,"* T. A. Blanco White.
[3] Reference may be made to standard works on company law.

It is sometimes of interest to stand back from a task of detail and to see it whole. Doing this, one may consider the question, in what frame of mind one should draft an agreement? Basically, it seems, there are two possible points of view. One may draft an agreement biasing it in every respect in one's own interest where latitude is possible, and leaving to the other party or his lawyers the task of modifying its rigour by counter-suggestions until a meeting point is reached. Alternatively, one may deliberately attempt to anticipate and meet objection, trying in all respects to be utterly fair and reasonable. It is not possible to say that one way is better than the other. It depends to some degree upon circumstances and the nature of the agreement. Even more, perhaps, it depends upon one's own view of the nature of business, upon one's own philosophy in the conduct of business life. Pasteur, in 1888, looking at the world around him, wrote:

> Two opposing laws seem to me now in contest. The one a law of blood and death, opening out each day new modes of destruction, forces nations to be always ready for battle. The other, a law of peace, work and health, whose only aim is to deliver man from the calamities that beset him. . . . Which of these two laws will prevail, God only knows.

How discerning his appraisal of the human situation was, the next three-quarters of a century were to show. Is it fanciful to see the same two laws working in business life? Certainly there are two kinds of businessmen, those who see business as a conflict and continuous struggle, and those who see it as the texture of economic co-operation. Perhaps the way we take in hand the matter of the drafting of an agreement shows which attitude expresses our personal philosophy. In professing a preference for the second way, that of the anticipations of objections and the quest for reasonableness, the author does no more than show that his own concept of business is that of co-operation rather than combat. But there certainly are the two techniques, and it is wise to be clear in one's own mind which of the two one is using, and to know why the choice has been made.

CONDITIONS OF SALE (A) FOR MACHINERY AND EQUIPMENT (EXCLUSIVE OF ERECTION) UNITED KINGDOM

(of British Electrical and Allied Manufacturers Association, 1967 Edition)

1. *GENERAL.*

The acceptance of our tender includes the acceptance of the following terms and conditions:

2. *VALIDITY.*

Unless previously withdrawn, our tender is open for acceptance within the period stated therein or, when no period is so stated, within thirty days only after its date.

3. *ACCEPTANCE.*

The acceptance of our tender must be accompanied by sufficient information to enable us to proceed with the order forthwith, otherwise we shall be at liberty to amend the tender prices to cover any increase in cost which has taken place after acceptance. Any samples submitted to you and not returned to our works within one month from date of receipt shall be paid for by you.

4. *PACKING.*

Unless otherwise specified in our tender, all packing cases, skids, drums and other packing materials must be returned to our works at your expense and in good condition within one month from date of receipt. If not so returned they will be charged for.

5. *LIMITS OF CONTRACT.*

Our tender includes only such goods, accessories and work as are specified therein.

6. *DRAWINGS, ETC.*

All specifications, drawings, and particulars of weights and dimensions submitted with our tender are approximate only, and the descriptions and illustrations contained in our catalogues, price lists and other advertisement matter are intended merely to present a general idea of the goods described therein, and none of these shall form part of the contract. After acceptance of our tender a set of certified outline drawings will be supplied free of charge on request.

7. *INSPECTION AND TESTS.*

Our products are carefully inspected and, where practicable, submitted to our standard tests at our works before despatch. If tests other than those specified in our tender or tests in the presence of you or your representative are required, these will be charged for. In the event of any delay on your part in attending such tests after seven days' notice that we are ready, the tests will proceed in your absence and shall be deemed to have been made in your presence.

8. *PERFORMANCE.*

We will accept no liability for failure to attain any performance figures quoted by us unless we have specifically guaranteed them, subject to any tolerances specified or agreed to by us, in an agreed sum as liquidated damages.

If the performance figures obtained on any test provided for in the contract are outside the rejection limits specified therein, you will be entitled to reject the goods.

Before you become entitled to claim liquidated damages or to reject the goods we are to be given reasonable time and opportunity to rectify their performance. If you become entitled to reject goods, we will repay to you any sum paid by you to us on account of the contract price thereof and any sum that may have accrued due to you in respect of delay in despatch under Clause 9 up to the date of such rejection.

You assume responsibility that goods stipulated by you are sufficient and suitable for your purpose save in so far as your stipulations are in accordance with our advice.

9. *LIABILITY FOR DELAY.*

Any times quoted for despatch or delivery are to date from receipt by us of a written order to proceed and of all necessary information and drawings to enable us to put the work in hand. The time for despatch or delivery shall be extended by a reasonable period if delay in despatch or delivery is caused by instructions or lack of instructions from you or by industrial dispute or by any cause beyond our reasonable control.

If a fixed time be quoted for despatch or delivery, and we fail to despatch or deliver within that time or within any extension thereof provided by this clause, and if as a result you shall have suffered loss, we undertake to pay for each week or part of a week of delay, liquidated damages at the rate of — per cent. up to a maximum of — per cent. of that portion of the price named in the contract which is referable to such portion only of the contract goods as cannot in consequence of the delay be used commercially and effectively. Such payment shall be in full satisfaction of our liability for delay.

Any time described as an estimate shall not be construed as a fixed time quoted for the purpose of this clause.

10. *VARIATIONS.*

In the event of variation or suspension of work by your instructions or lack of instructions the contract price shall be adjusted accordingly.

11. *DELIVERY.*

Unless otherwise specified in our tender, the price quoted includes delivery by any method of transport at our option within the free rail delivery area. If transport is by rail the General Conditions of Carriage of the British Railways' Board shall apply.

Unless otherwise specified, we shall not be responsible for offloading.

12. *LOSS OR DAMAGE IN TRANSIT.*

When the price quoted includes delivery other than at our works, we will repair or at our option replace free of charge goods lost or damaged in transit; Provided that we are given written notification of such loss or damage within such time as will enable us to comply with the carrier's conditions of carriage as affecting loss or damage in transit or, where delivery is made by our own transport, within a reasonable time after receipt of the Advice Note.

13. *TERMS OF PAYMENT.*

Unless otherwise agreed, payment in full shall be due for goods on notification by us that they are ready for despatch.

14. *STORAGE.*

If we do not receive forwarding instructions sufficient to enable us to despatch the goods within 14 days after the date of notification that they are ready for despatch, you shall take delivery or arrange for storage.   If you do not take delivery or arrange for storage, we shall be entitled to arrange storage either at our own works or elsewhere on your behalf and all charges for storage, for insurance or for demurrage shall be payable by you.

15. *DEFECTS AFTER DELIVERY*.

We will make good, by repair or at our option by the supply of a replacement, defects which under proper use appear in the goods within a period of twelve calendar months after the goods have been delivered and arise solely from faulty design, materials or workmanship; Provided always that defective parts are promptly returned by you free to our works unless otherwise arranged.   The repaired or new parts will be delivered by us free of charge as provided in Clause 11.

Our liability under this clause shall be in lieu of any warranty or condition implied by law as to the quality or fitness for any particular purpose of the goods, and save as provided in this clause we shall not be under any liability, whether in contract, tort or otherwise, in respect of defects in goods delivered or for any injury, damage or loss resulting from such defects or from any work done in connection therewith.

16. *PATENTS.*

We will indemnify you against any claim for infringement of Letters Patent, Registered Design, Trade Mark or Copyright (published at the date of the contract) by the use or sale of any article or material supplied by us to you and against all costs and damages which you may incur in any action for such infringement or for which you may become liable in any such action.   Provided always that this indemnity shall not apply to any infringement which is due to our having followed a design or instruction furnished or given by you or to the use of such article or material in a manner or for a purpose or in a foreign country not specified by or disclosed to us, or to any infringement which is due to the use of such article or material in association or combination with any other article or material not supplied by us.   And provided

o

also that this indemnity is conditional on your giving to us the earliest possible notice in writing of any claim being made or action threatened or brought against you and on your permitting us at our own expense to conduct any litigation that may ensue and all negotiations for a settlement of the claim. You on your part warrant that any design or instruction furnished or given by you shall not be such as will cause us to infringe any Letters Patent, Registered Design, Trade Mark or Copyright in the execution of your order.

17. *LIABILITY FOR ACCIDENTS AND DAMAGE.*

If we, our agents or sub-contractors are on site for the purposes of the contract then, notwithstanding the provisions of Clause 15 we will indemnify you against direct damage or injury to your property or person or that of others occurring while we are working on site to the extent caused by the negligence of ourselves, our sub-contractors or agents, but not otherwise, by making good such damage to property or compensating personal injury. Provided that:

(a) our total liability for damage to your property shall not exceed £50,000 or the contract price, whichever sum is the greater, and—

(b) we shall not be liable to you for any loss of profit or of contracts or, save as aforesaid, for any loss, damage or injury of any kind whatsoever.

Save as provided in Clause 15, we shall not be liable for any damage or injury occurring after our completion of work on site.

18. *FAIR WAGES CLAUSE.*

We undertake to be bound by a fair wages clause in the terms of the House of Commons Resolution of October 14, 1946. We also undertake that when the installation of machinery and equipment is carried out by men sent from the Contractor's or Sub-Contractor's establishment they shall receive the time rate payable in terms of the Fair Wages Clause to such workpeople in such establishment, and in addition shall receive the outworking allowances recognised for outworkers sent from such establishment.

19. *ARBITRATION.*

If at any time any question, dispute or difference whatsoever shall arise between you and ourselves upon, in relation to, or in connection with the contract, either of us may give to the other notice in writing of the existence of such question, dispute, or difference, and the same shall be referred to the arbitration of a person to be mutually agreed upon, or failing agreement within 14 days of receipt of such notice, of some person appointed by the President for the time being of the Institution of Electrical Engineers.

20. *LEGAL CONSTRUCTION.*

Unless otherwise agreed in writing the contract shall in all respects be construed and operate as an English contract and in conformity with English law.

PURCHASING OFFICERS ASSOCIATION, TERMS AND CONDITIONS OF CONTRACT, 1960 EDITION

Draft Model Standard Conditions of Contract

Clause 1—*Definitions*

" Buyer " means ....

" Seller " means the person, firm or company to whom the Order is addressed.

" Goods " means the articles or things or any of them described in the Order.

" Specification " means the technical description (if any) of the Goods contained or referred to in the Order.

" Order " means the order placed by the Buyer for the supply of the goods.

Clause 2—*Acknowledgment*

The Buyer shall be bound by his Order only
  (i) if it is placed on his official order form;
  (ii) if the Seller accepts it in writing within — [1] days of the date of the Order.

Clause 3—*Variations*

(i) Neither the Buyer nor the Seller shall be bound by any variation, waiver of, or addition to these Conditions except as agreed by both parties in writing and signed on their behalf.

Clause 4—*Quality and Description*

Subject to Clauses 10 and 11 the Goods shall:
  (i) conform as to quantity, quality, and description with the particulars stated in the Order;
  (ii) be of sound materials and workmanship;
  (iii) be equal in all respect to the samples, patterns, or specification provided or given by either party;
  (iv) be capable of any standard of performance specified in the Order;

---

[1] Insert number of days.

    (v) if the purpose for which they are required is indicated in the Order either expressly or by implication, be fit for that purpose.

Clause 5—*Inspection and Testing*

    (i) Before despatching the Goods the Seller shall carefully inspect and test them for compliance with the Specification. The Seller shall, if requested by the Buyer, give the buyer reasonable notice of such tests and the Buyer shall be entitled to be represented thereat. The Seller shall also, at the request of the Buyer, supply to the Buyer a copy of the Seller's test sheets certified by the Seller to be a true copy.

    (ii) If it is expressly agreed the Buyer will be entitled to inspect and test the Goods during manufacture, processing, or storage. If the Buyer exercises this right, the Seller shall provide or shall procure the provision of all such facilities as may reasonably be required by the Buyer therefor.

    (iii) If as a result of any inspection or test under paragraphs (i) or (ii) of this Clause the Buyer's representative is of the reasonable opinion that the Goods do not comply with the Order, or are unlikely on completion of manufacture or processing so to comply he shall inform the Seller accordingly in writing and the Seller shall take such steps as may be necessary to ensure such compliance.

Clause 6—*Delivery*

    (i) The Goods, properly packed and secured in such a manner as to reach their destination in good condition under normal conditions of transport, shall be delivered by the Seller at, or despatched for delivery to, the place or places and in the manner specified in the Order or as subsequently agreed.

    (ii) Arrangements for payment and return of returnable wooden packing cases, skids, drums, and other reusable articles used for packing the Goods will be as specified in the Order.

Clause 7—Storage

If for any reason the Buyer is unable to accept delivery of the Goods at the time when the Goods are due and ready for delivery the Seller shall, if his storage facilities permit, store the Goods, safeguard them, and take all reasonable steps to prevent their deterioration until their actual delivery, and the Buyer shall be liable to the Seller for the reasonable cost (including insurance) of his so doing.

Clause 8—Passing of Property

(i) Subject to the provisions of paragraph (ii) of this Clause the property in the Goods shall pass to the Buyer on delivery without prejudice to any right of rejection which may accrue to the Buyer under these Conditions.

(ii) If the Seller postpones delivery at the request of the Buyer pursuant to Clause 7 the property in the Goods shall pass to the Buyer seven days after the date of receipt of notification from the Seller that the Goods are due and ready for delivery or on such other date as may be agreed but the goods shall nevertheless remain at the Seller's risk until delivery has been completed.

Clause 9—Time

(i) The Seller shall deliver the Goods at the time specified in the Order. Time shall begin to run from the date of acceptance by the Seller of the Order or the date on which the Seller is placed in possession of such information and drawings as may be necessary to enable him to start work on the Goods, whichever may be the later. If owing to industrial disputes or any causes outside the Seller's control the Seller is unable to deliver the Goods within the specified time then provided that the Seller shall have given the Buyer notice in writing without delay of his intention to claim an extension of time the Buyer shall grant the Seller such extension of time as may be reasonable.

(ii) If the Goods or any portion thereof are not delivered within the time or times specified in the Contract or any extension of such time or times, the Buyer shall be entitled to determine the Contract in respect of the Goods undelivered as aforesaid and of any other goods already delivered under the Contract which cannot be effectively and commercially used by reason of the non-delivery of the goods undelivered as aforesaid. On such determination the Buyer shall be entitled:

(a) to return to the Seller at the Seller's risk and expense any of the Goods already delivered but which cannot be effectively and commercially used as aforesaid and to recover from the Seller any moneys paid by the Buyer in respect of such Goods;

(b) to recover from the Seller any additional expenditure reasonably incurred by the Buyer in obtaining other goods in replacement of those in respect of which the Contract has been determined.

(iii) If the parties have expressly so agreed but not otherwise the provisions hereinafter set out in this sub-clause shall apply in lieu of sub-clause (ii) above.

If the Goods or any portion thereof are not delivered within the time or times specified in the Contract or any extension of such time or times, the Buyer may recover from the Seller as liquidated damages, and not by way of penalty, — [2] per cent. of that part of the contract price which is properly apportionable to the goods undelivered as aforesaid (hereinafter in this sub-clause referred to as " Undelivered Goods ") and to any other goods already delivered under the Contract which cannot be effectively and commercially used by reason of the non-delivery of the Undelivered Goods for each week during which such failure continues. Provided that the sum so recoverable shall not exceed — [2] per cent. of the contract price and shall be in full satisfaction of the Seller's liability for such failure.

[2] The appropriate percentage to be inserted.

Clause 10—*Rejection*

    (i) The Buyer may by notice in writing to the Seller reject the Goods if the Seller fails to comply with his obligations under Clause 5 hereof and may also by notice in writing to the Seller given within twenty-eight days or such other period as may be agreed after delivery, reject any Goods which are found not to be in accordance with the Contract.

    (ii) The Buyer shall when giving notice of rejection specify the reasons therefor and shall thereafter return the rejected Goods to the Seller at the Seller's risk and expense. In such case the Seller shall within a reasonable time replace such rejected Goods with goods which are in all respects in accordance with the Contract.

    (iii) Any money paid by the Buyer to the Seller in respect of any rejected Goods not replaced by the Seller within a reasonable time together with any additional expenditure over and above the Contract Price reasonably incurred by the Buyer in obtaining other goods in replacement shall be paid by the Seller to the Buyer.

Clause 11—*Guarantee*

    (i) If within the period after delivery named in the Order (hereinafter called " the Guarantee Period ") the Buyer gives notice in writing to the Seller of any defect in the Goods which shall arise under proper use from faulty design (other than a design made, furnished, or specified by the Buyer for which the Seller has in writing disclaimed responsibility), materials, or workmanship, then the Seller shall with all possible speed replace or repair the Goods so as to remedy the defects without cost to the Buyer.

    (ii) The Buyer shall, as soon as practicable after discovering any such defect or failure, return the defective Goods or parts thereof to the Seller and at the Seller's risk and expense unless it has been agreed between the Parties that the necessary replacement or repair shall be carried out by the Seller on the Buyer's premises.

(iii) Notwithstanding anything in Clause 4 the Seller shall be under no liability to the Buyer in respect of loss of or defects in Goods supplied except as specified in Clauses 10 and 12 and this Clause, nor subject as aforesaid shall he be liable for any personal injury, damage, or loss of any kind attributable to such loss of, or defects in, such Goods.

Clause 12—Damage or Loss in Transit

The Seller will repair or replace, free of charge, Goods damaged or lost in transit provided the Buyer shall give the Seller written notification of such damage or loss within such time as will enable the Seller to comply with the carrier's conditions of carriage, as affecting loss or damage in transit, or where delivery is made by the Seller's own transport, within a reasonable time.

Clause 13—Payment

Payment of the Price shall be made within the period after delivery specified in the Order, or if delivery is postponed at the request of the Buyer as provided in Clause 7 within the same period after the date when the property in the Goods passed to the Buyer under that Clause.

Clause 14—Care and Return of Patterns, Dies, etc.

(i) All patterns, dies, moulds, or other tooling supplied by the Buyer or prepared or obtained by the Seller for and at the sole cost of the Buyer, shall be and remain the property of the Buyer.

(ii) The Seller shall maintain all such items in good order and condition and insure them against all risks whilst in his custody and on completion of the contract or as otherwise directed by the Buyer shall return them to the Buyer in good order and condition. Should the Seller fail so to return them the Buyer may either withhold payment until they are so returned or withhold such part of the payment due as may be required to replace them or to restore them to good order and condition, whichever may be the less expensive.

(iii) The Seller shall not use such items, nor shall he

authorise or knowingly permit them to be used by anyone else for, or in connection with, any purpose other than the supply of the Goods to the Buyer unless such use is expressly authorised by the Buyer, previously and in writing.

Clause 15—Insurance of Buyer's Goods, etc.

The Seller shall insure any material or property sent to the Seller by the Buyer for any purpose in connection with the contract against any damage which may occur to it whilst in his custody.

Clause 16—Statutory Requirements

The Seller warrants that the design, construction, and quality of goods to be supplied under the contract comply in all respects with all relevant requirements of any Statute, Statutory Rule or Order, or other instrument having the force of law which may be in force at the time when the same are supplied.

Clause 17—Infringement of Patents

(i) The Seller shall fully indemnify the Buyer against any action, claim, demand, costs, charges, and expenses arising from or incurred by reason of any infringement or alleged infringement of any letters patent, registered design, trade mark, or trade name protected in the United Kingdom by the use or sale of the goods and against all costs and damages which the Buyer may incur in any action for such infringement or for which the Buyer may become liable in any such action. Provided always that this indemnity shall not apply to any infringement which is due to the Seller having followed a design or instruction furnished by the Buyer or to the use of the goods in a manner or for a purpose not reasonably to be inferred by the Seller or disclosed to the Seller prior to the making of the Contract.

(ii) In the event of any claim being made or action brought against the Buyer arising out of the matters referred to in this clause, the Seller shall be promptly notified thereof and may at his own expense conduct all negotiations for the settlement of the same, and any litigation that may arise therefrom. The Buyer shall not, unless and until the Seller shall have failed to take over the conduct of the negotiations or litigation, make any admission which might be prejudicial thereto. The conduct by the Seller of such negotiations or litigation shall be conditional upon the Seller having first given to the Buyer such reasonable security as shall from time to time be required by the Buyer to cover the amount ascertained or agreed or estimated, as the case may be, of any compensation, damages, expenses, and costs for which the Buyer may become liable. The Buyer shall, at the request of the Seller, afford all available assistance for any such purpose, and shall be repaid any expenses incurred in so doing.

(iii) The Buyer on his part warrants that any design or instructions furnished or given by him shall not be such as will cause the Seller to infringe any letters patent, registered design, trade mark, or trade name in the performance of the Contract.

Clause 18—*Assignment and Sub-Contracting*

(i) The seller shall not without the consent in writing of the Buyer assign or transfer the Contract or any part of it to any other person except as part of a company amalgamation or reconstruction.

(ii) The Seller shall not without the consent in writing of the Buyer sub-let the Contract or any part thereof other than for materials, minor details, or for any part of the Goods of which the makers are named in the Order or the Specification, but this shall not prevent the Seller sub-letting part of the Contract to any company which is a member of the group to which the Seller belongs or a company with whom the Seller is associated. Any such consent shall not relieve the Seller of any of his obligations under the Contract.

Clause 19—*Bankruptcy or Liquidation*

(i) If the Seller being an individual (or, when the Seller

is a firm, any partner in that firm) shall at any time become bankrupt, or shall have a receiving order or administration order made against him or shall make any composition or arrangement with, or for the benefit of his creditors, or shall make any conveyance or assignment for the benefit of his creditors or shall purport to do so, or if in Scotland he shall become insolvent or notour bankrupt, or any application shall be made under any Bankruptcy Act for the time being in force for sequestration of his estate, or a trust deed shall be granted by him on behalf of his creditors, or if the Seller, being a Company, shall pass a resolution, or the Court shall make an order that the Company shall be wound up (not being a Members' winding up for the purpose of reconstruction or amalgamation) or if a receiver, or manager on behalf of a creditor shall be appointed, or if circumstances shall arise which entitle the Court or a creditor to appoint a receiver or manager, or which entitle the Court to make a winding-up order, then the Buyer shall be at liberty:

    (a) to cancel the Order summarily by notice in writing without compensation to the Seller, or

    (b) to give any such receiver or liquidator or other person the option of carrying out the contract.

(ii) The exercise of any of the rights granted to the Buyer under paragraph (i) hereof shall not prejudice or affect any right of action or remedy which shall have accrued or shall accrue thereafter to the Buyer.

Clause 20—*Indemnity*

(i) The Seller shall subject to sub-clauses (ii) and (iii) and (iv) of this clause indemnify the Buyer in respect of all damage or injury occurring before the expiry of the Guarantee Period to any person or to any property and against all actions, suits, claims, demands, costs, charges, or expenses arising in connection therewith to the extent that the same shall have been occasioned by the negligence of the Seller, his servants or agents during such time as he or they were on, entering on to, or departing from the Buyer's premises for any purpose connected with the Contract.

(ii) The Seller shall not be liable to the Buyer for:
  (a) any loss of profit or of contracts,
  (b) any damage or injury to the extent that the same is caused by or arises out of the acts or omissions of the Buyer or of others (not being the Seller's servants or agents).

(iii) In the event of any claim being made against the Buyer by reason of any matter referred to and in respect of which the Seller is liable under this clause the Seller shall be promptly notified thereof and may at his own expense conduct all negotiations for the settlement of the same and any litigation that may arise therefrom. The Buyer shall not unless and until the Seller shall have failed to take over the conduct of the negotiations or litigations make any admission which might be prejudicial thereto. The conduct by the Seller of such negotiations or litigation shall be conditional upon the Contractor having first given to the Buyer such reasonable security as shall from time to time be required by the Buyer to cover the amount ascertained, or agreed, or estimated as the case may be, of any compensation, damages, expenses, and costs for which the Buyer may become liable. The Buyer shall at the request of the Seller afford all available assistance for any such purpose and shall be repaid any out of pocket expenses incurred in so doing.

(iv) Except in respect of personal injury or damage to property conferring on a person other than the Buyer a good cause of action against the Seller, the liability of the Seller to the Buyer for any one act or default shall not exceed the sum named on the Order or if no such sum is named the Contract Price.

Clause 21—*Arbitration*

All disputes, differences, or questions at any time arising between the parties as to the construction of the Contract or as to any matter or thing arising out of the Contract or in any way connected therewith shall be referred to the arbitration of a single arbitrator who shall be agreed between the parties or who failing such agreement shall be appointed at the request of either party in the case of an English contract by the President for the time being of the Law Society, and in the case of a Scottish contract by the President for the time being of the Law Society of Scotland. The arbitration shall be in accordance with the Arbitration Act 1950 in the case of an English Contract.

Clause 22—Law of the Contract

Unless otherwise agreed the Contract shall be subject to English **Law.**

Additional Clauses not covered in the Standard Conditions

Price Variation

As drafted the Standard Conditions assume that the price of the Goods is fixed and not subject to price rise and fall. In practice, however, Purchasing Officers may find that under present conditions they do have to accept price rise and fall clauses as part of the Contract. The following notes are given as a guide to Purchasing Officers in negotiating such clauses:

(i) The contract price must be related to a certain date, usually the date of the Seller's quotation.

(ii) Labour rates should be tied to a nationally recognised wage regulating body so that only awards of that body are taken into account.

(iii) Material costs should be related to a definite list of materials and the Seller should be required when quoting to state the basic price of those materials as on the date of his quotation.

(iv) Even when the information listed above is available it may be very difficult in the absence of a formula to translate increases which have occurred to material and labour costs into a variation of the contract price. It is common therefore to use a formula in which a percentage of the contract price representing overheads and profits is regarded as fixed, a percentage varies with labour and a percentage with specified material costs. The two most important points in connection with such a formula are: the percentage which is regarded as fixed, this is commonly around 20 per cent. and how the variation is to be adjusted depending upon in which period of the Contract the rise or fall occurs.

Erection on Site

The Standard Conditions of Contract set out above are only intended for use where the contract is one for supply only. In many instances, however, the Buyer will want the Seller to at least help with or supervise erection or installation of the goods if not actually carry out such erection or installation. If the Seller's responsibilities are to be extended in this way then the following points will require consideration:

When should payment of the contract price be made? It is suggested that a convenient method is to be a percentage of the contract price for the goods, around 90 per cent. on completion of delivery, the balance of this price plus the erection charges on completion of erection.

The limit on the indemnity clause will need to be considered very carefully since carelessness of the Seller's staff engaged on the erection work could be very costly.

MODEL FORM OF GENERAL CONDITIONS OF CONTRACT (C)
1956 EDITION

Model Form of General Conditions of Contract Recommended by the Institution of Mechanical Engineers and the Institution of Electrical Engineers for the sale of Electrical and Mechanical Goods, other than Electric Cables (Home – Without Erection)

General Conditions

1. These General Conditions shall have effect subject to any express stipulation or condition at variance with these Conditions that may be contained in the Specification or may otherwise be incorporated in the Contract.

Information

2. The Purchaser shall within a reasonable time furnish all such further information, beyond that which is contained in the Specification or has been otherwise given to the Vendor, as the Vendor may reasonably call for to execute the Contract. The Purchaser shall pay all reasonable extra costs caused to the Vendor by unreasonable delay in supplying information reasonably called for by the Vendor or by the supply of inaccurate information.

Drawings

3. (i) Drawings, illustrations, descriptions, price lists, and catalogues issued by the Vendor shall not form part of the Contract unless incorporated therein by reference or otherwise.

(ii) The Vendor shall within a reasonable time supply to the Purchaser –

    (a) the particulars and drawings (if any) called for in the Contract, and

    (b) such drawings (other than shop drawings) and other particulars of the goods as may be reasonably necessary for the purposes of installation and maintenance (including such dismantling and reassembling as maintenance may involve).

Tests

4. (i) Before delivering any goods the Vendor shall inspect and test the same for compliance with the Contract and, if so requested shall supply to the Purchaser a certificate of the results of the tests.

(ii) Where the Contract provides that the goods shall pass any prescribed tests or shall give a specified performance they shall be tested by the Vendor before delivery for compliance with the prescribed tests or for performance or for both as the case may be, the Vendor providing free of charge what may be requisite for the purpose. The Vendor shall give the Purchaser seven days' notice in writing of the date on and the place at which any of the goods will be ready for testing as provided in this Sub-clause. If the Purchaser shall fail to give the Vendor twenty-four hours' notice appointing a day within seven days after the date which the Vendor has stated in his notice, or shall fail to attend on the day he has appointed, the Vendor may proceed with the tests, which shall be deemed to have been made in the Purchaser's presence. The Vendor shall forthwith forward to the Purchaser a certificate of the results of the test.

(iii) If on a test made pursuant to Sub-clause (ii) of this clause the goods or any part thereof fail to pass the prescribed tests or to give the specified performance such goods or part thereof shall, if the Vendor so desires, be tested again or the Vendor may submit for test other goods in their place. If the goods or the said other goods shall fail to pass the test or to give the specified performance, the Purchaser shall be entitled by notice in writing to reject the goods or such part thereof as shall have failed as aforesaid.

Rejection and Replacement

5. (i) The Purchaser shall be entitled, by notice in writing given within a reasonable time after delivery, to reject goods delivered which are not in accordance with the Contract.

(ii) When goods have been rejected, either under Clause 4 (Tests) or Sub-clause (i) of this clause, the Purchaser shall be entitled, provided he does so without undue delay, to replace the goods so rejected. There shall be deducted from the

Contract Price that part thereof which is properly apportionable to the goods rejected. The Vendor shall pay to the Purchaser any sum by which the expenditure reasonably incurred by the Purchaser in replacing the rejected goods exceeds the sum deducted. All goods obtained by the Purchaser to replace rejected goods shall comply with the Contract and shall be obtained at reasonable prices and, when reasonably practicable, under competitive conditions. Where goods have been rejected, the Vendor shall not be under any liability to the Purchaser in respect of the circumstances which have given rise to the right to reject, except as provided in this clause and as may arise under Clause 7 (Time for Delivery).

Place of Delivery

6. The Vendor shall deliver the goods at the place (if any) named in the Contract or, if none be named, at the Vendor's works. Where delivery is to be made otherwise than at the Vendor's works the Vendor shall convey the goods to the point nearest to the place of delivery to which there is suitable access and the Purchaser shall be responsible for unloading the goods. Where delivery is to be made at the Vendor's works the Vendor shall, if required, load the goods on the Purchaser's vehicle.

Time for Delivery

7. (i) Any time fixed by the Contract for delivery shall run from the acceptance of the Vendor's tender (or, if there be no tender, of the Purchaser's order) or from the date on which the Vendor is placed by the Purchaser in possession of such information and drawings as may be necessary to enable him to put the work in hand, whichever may be the later. Any time described as an estimate shall not be construed as a time fixed by the Contract.

(ii) If for any cause beyond the reasonable control of the Vendor or by reason of any industrial dispute delivery of the goods shall be delayed the above-mentioned time for delivery shall be extended by such period as may be reasonable.

(iii) If the Purchaser shall have suffered any loss by the failure of the Vendor to deliver goods in accordance with the Contract within the time fixed thereby or, if no time be fixed, within a reasonable time, the Purchaser shall be entitled to recover liquidated damages from the Vendor. Such damages shall be a sum equal to the percentage specified in the Contract or that part of the Contract Price which is properly apportionable to such portion of the goods as cannot in consequence of such failure be put to the use intended for each week until the Vendor has delivered goods in accordance with the Contract, or goods in replacement have been provided by the Purchaser pursuant to Sub-clause (ii) of Clause 5 (Rejection and Replacement). Provided always that the amount so recoverable shall not exceed the maximum percentage specified in the Contract of the Contract Price. In default of specification in the Contract the percentages above mentioned shall be $\frac{1}{2}$ per cent. and 10 per cent. respectively.

(iv) When the sum recoverable by the Purchaser as liquidated damages has amounted to the maximum above provided the Purchaser shall be entitled by notice in writing to the Vendor to require him to deliver the goods within such time (not being less than twenty-eight days) as the Purchaser may specify in the notice. If the Vendor shall fail to deliver the goods within the time so specified the Purchaser shall, without prejudice to his rights under Sub-clause (iii) of this clause, be entitled, after having informed the Vendor in writing of his intention to do so, to obtain goods in place of those which the Vendor has failed to deliver and there shall be deducted from the Contract Price that part thereof which is properly apportionable to the undelivered goods. The Vendor shall pay to the Purchaser any sum by which the expenditure reasonably incurred by the Purchaser in obtaining goods in place of undelivered goods exceeds the sum deducted. All goods obtained by the purchaser in place of undelivered goods shall comply with the Contract and shall be obtained at reasonable prices and when practicable under competitive conditions.

(v) The Purchaser's remedies under Sub-clauses (iii) and (iv) of this clause shall be in lieu of any other remedy in respect of the Vendor's failure to deliver goods in accordance with the Contract within the time fixed thereby or, if no time be fixed, within a reasonable time.

Storage

8. If by reason of instructions or lack of instructions from the Purchaser the despatch of goods in accordance with the

Contract is delayed for fourteen days after the Vendor has given notice in writing to the Purchaser that the said goods are ready for despatch, the said goods shall be deemed to have been delivered in accordance with the Contract and thereafter, subject as provided in Clause 9 (Damage or Loss in Transit), the goods shall be deemed to be at the risk of the Purchaser. Nevertheless the Vendor shall use his best endeavours to deliver the said goods in accordance with such instructions as may be given to him by the Purchaser and in the meantime to store, protect, preserve, and, if required by the Purchaser, insure them to the extent so required. The Purchaser shall repay to the Vendor the reasonable cost of so storing, protecting, preserving, and insuring the said goods.

Damage or loss in transit

9. (i) The Vendor shall repair or replace free of charge goods damaged in transit to the place of delivery, and in the event of such damage delivery shall not be deemed to have taken place until repaired or replacement goods have been delivered. Provided always that, if the Vendor has given to the Purchaser notice of the date of despatch and has with that notice required the Purchaser to give him within a stated period notice of any damage suffered and the Purchaser has failed to do so, the Vendor shall not be liable to repair or replace the damaged goods, and delivery of the damaged goods shall be deemed to be delivery for the purpose of the Contract. For the purposes of this sub-clause the stated period shall –

(a) where the goods are delivered by a carrier employed by the Vendor under a contract of carriage which frees the carrier from liability for damage in transit unless notice of damage is given to the carrier within a specified time, be such a period (not being less than twenty-four hours) after the receipt of the goods as will allow the Vendor at least twenty-four hours after receiving notice from the Purchaser within which to give notice to the carrier in compliance with the terms of the carrier's said contract with the Vendor, and

(b) where the goods are delivered by a carrier employed by the Vendor but not under such a contract as aforesaid or are delivered by the Vendor's own transport, be such a period as is reasonable.

(ii) The Vendor shall replace goods lost in transit to the place of delivery provided always that, if the Vendor has given the Purchaser notice of the date of despatch and method of transport and has with that notice required the Purchaser to give him notice of non-delivery within a stated period and the Purchaser has failed to do so, the goods shall notwithstanding their non-receipt within that period be deemed to have been delivered at the expiry of that period. In such last mentioned event the Vendor shall at the request and expense of the Purchaser pursue for the benefit of the Purchaser such rights (if any) as the Vendor may have against the carrier.

(iii) The liability imposed on the Vendor in this clause shall be accepted by the Purchaser in substitution for all or any other liability on the part of the Vendor arising from the delivery of goods damaged in transit or the non-delivery of goods in consequence of loss in transit.

Terms of payment

10. Unless otherwise agreed, payment for the goods shall become due on completion of delivery in accordance with the Contract.

Defects after delivery

11. (i) If within twelve months after delivery there shall appear in the goods any defect which shall arise under the proper use from faulty design (other than a design made, furnished, or specified by the Purchaser for which the Vendor has in writing disclaimed responsibility), materials, or workmanship and the Purchaser shall give notice thereof in writing to the Vendor, the Vendor shall, provided that the defective goods or defective parts thereof have been returned to the Vendor if he shall have so required, make good the defects either by repair or, at the option of the Vendor, by the supply of a replacement. The Vendor shall refund the cost of carriage on return of the defective goods or parts and shall deliver any repaired or replacement goods or parts as if Clause 6 (Place of Delivery) applied.

(ii) The Vendor's liability under this clause or under Clause 5 (Rejection and Replacement) shall be accepted by the Purchaser in lieu of any liability, whether under any warranty or condition express or implied by law or otherwise, in respect of the quality or the design or the fitness for any particular purpose of the goods.

Patents and design

12. (i) The Vendor shall fully indemnify the Purchaser against any action, claim, demand, costs, charges, and expenses arising from or incurred by reason of any infringement or alleged infringement of any letters patent, registered design, trade mark, or trade name protected in the United Kingdom by the use or sale of the goods and against all costs and damages which the Purchaser may incur in any action for such infringement or for which the Purchaser may become liable in any such action. Provided always that this indemnity shall not apply to any infringement which is due to the Vendor having followed a design or instruction furnished by the Purchaser or to the use of the goods in a manner or for a purpose not reasonably to be inferred by the Vendor instructions furnished or given by him shall not be such as will or disclosed to the Vendor prior to the making of the Contract.

(ii) In the event of any claim being made or action brought against the Purchaser arising out of the matters referred to in this clause, the Vendor shall be promptly notified thereof and may at his own expense conduct all negotiations for the settlement of the same, and any limitation that may arise therefrom. The Purchaser shall not, unless and until the Vendor shall have failed to take over the conduct of the negotiations or litigation, make any admission which might be prejudiced thereto. The conduct by the Vendor of such negotiations or litigation shall be conditional upon the Vendor having first given to the Purchaser such reasonable security as shall from time to time be required by the Purchaser to cover the amount ascertained or agreed or estimated, as the case may be, of any compensation, damages, expenses, and costs for which the Purchaser may become liable. The Purchaser shall, at the request of the Vendor, afford all available assistance for any such purpose, and shall be repaid

(iii) The Purchaser on his part warrants that any design or any expenses incurred in so doing.

cause the Vendor to infringe any letters patent, registered design, trade mark, or trade names in the performance of the Contract.

Arbitration

13. If at any time any question, dispute, or difference whatsoever shall arise between the Vendor and the Purchaser upon, in relation to, or in connection with the Contract, either of them shall give to the other notice in writing of the existence of such question, dispute, or difference, and the same shall be referred to the arbitration of a person to be agreed upon or failing agreement within fourteen days after the date of such notice, of some person to be appointed, on the application of either party, by the President for the time being of The Institution of [1] Engineers.

Italic headings

14. The italic headings hereto shall not affect the construction hereof.

Supplementary Clause (optional)

Variations in costs and tax fluctuations

(i) If, by reason of any rise or fall in the rates of wages payable to labour or in the cost of material or transport or of conforming to such laws, orders, regulations and by-laws as are applicable to the Works above or below such rates and costs ruling at the date of the tender, the cost to the Contractor of performing his obligations under this Contract shall be increased or reduced, the amount of such increase or reduction shall be added to or deducted from the Contract Price as the case may be, provided that no account shall be taken of any amount by which any cost incurred by the Contractor has been increased by the default or negligence of the Contractor. For the purposes of this clause " the cost of material " shall be construed as including any duty or tax by whomsoever payable which is payable under or by virtue of any Act of Parliament on the import, purchase, sale, appropriation, processing or use of such material.

(ii) If, as a result of the coming into effect after the date of the tender of any change in the level or in the incidence of any labour-tax matter, including the imposition of any new such matter, or the abolition of any such matter previously existing,

[1] Insert Mechanical or Electrical as preferred.

the cost to the Contractor of performing his obligations under the Contract shall be increased or reduced, the amount of such increase or reduction shall be added to or deducted from the Contract price as the case may be.

In this sub-clause " labour-tax matter " means any tax levy or contribution (including National Insurance contributions but excluding Income Tax and any levy payable under the Industrial Training Act 1964) which is by law payable by the Contractor in respect of labour and any premiums and refunds which are by law payable to the Contractor in respect of labour.

(iii) The Contractor may incorporate in any sub-contract made for the purpose of performing his obligations under the Contract, provisions which are *mutatis mutandis* the same as the provisions of this clause and in such event the addition or deduction to be made in accordance with any sub-contract shall also be made under the Contract as if the increase or decrease of cost to the Sub-contractor had been directly incurred by the Contractor.

INDEX

217